WIRING PROJECTS
FOR YOUR MODEL RAILROAD

Larry Puckett

WAUKESHA, WI

Kalmbach Books
21027 Crossroads Circle
Waukesha, Wisconsin 53186
www.KalmbachHobbyStore.com

Published in 2018
22 21 20 19 18   1 2 3 4 5

Manufactured in China

ISBN: 978-1-62700-502-9
EISBN: 978-1-62700-503-6

Editor: Jeff Wilson
Book Design: Tom Ford

Unless noted, photographs were taken by the author.

Library of Congress Control Number: 2017941411

Contents

Introduction
Improve operation and layout realism 4

Chapter 1
Light bulbs and LEDs 6

Chapter 2
Lighting small structures 10

Chapter 3
Lighting a large structure 15

Chapter 4
Animated neon signs 20

Chapter 5
Crossbucks and flashing signals 25

Chapter 6
Crossing gates 32

Chapter 7
Working interlocking semaphore signal 38

Chapter 8
Installing and wiring a turntable 43

Chapter 9
Electromagnetic uncouplers 47

Chapter 10
Adding and wiring a lift-out bridge 51

Chapter 11
DC controls for switch machines 55

Chapter 12
Control panel with pushbuttons 60

Chapter 13
Install a track scale with LED display 65

Chapter 14
Install a working telephone system 69

Chapter 15
Add a fast clock for operations 77

Chapter 16
Build a magnetic dispatcher's panel 84

Appendices
Basics of soldering 92

List of manufacturers 94

About the author 95

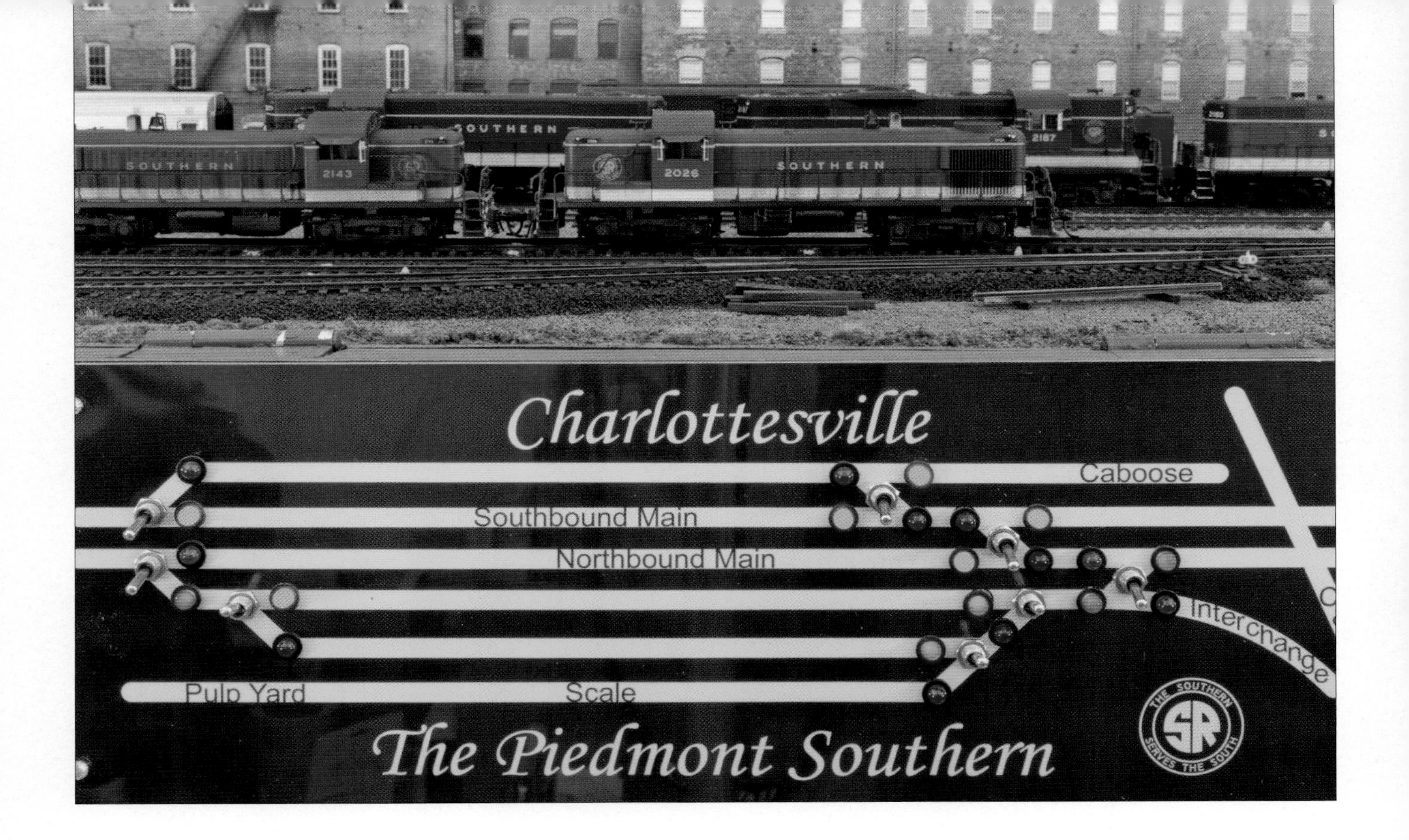

INTRODUCTION

Improve operations and layout realism

Control panels help operators by providing a visual reinforcement of turnout locations, with toggle or pushbutton switches controlling switch machines. Panels can also include indicator lights and other features. Chapters 11, 12, and 16 provide more details.

Model railroading is a great hobby that constantly challenges us to learn new approaches and methods for creating realistic operating railroads in miniature. In this book I will walk you through a number of projects that will not only add to the realism of your layout but also make it easier and more enjoyable to operate.

Structure interior and exterior lighting, along with detail lights, provide a great deal of visual interest to any scene. Chapters 1 through 4 provide many examples.

Over my 35-plus years in the hobby I've encountered many prototype details, either through photographs or in person, that I knew I wanted to feature on my layout. This book is a selection of some of those projects. Some are relatively easy and others complex, but I believe all are within the reach of most modelers.

Most model railroad projects aren't that difficult, even if they seem so at first. The key is breaking things down into steps. The most important step in developing a project is to define exactly what it is you want to achieve. Once you get that part solved it then becomes a matter of finding the materials and components required.

This is the part that is often the most difficult. For example, for several years I knew I wanted a working telephone system, but it wasn't until Seth Neumann came along with his telephone network circuit board and professional knowledge of telephone systems that I was able to put it all together.

I've tried to do this step for you, and each chapter will provide instructions on putting everything together. Even if you want something a little different than what I have done, I hope my experiences will get you moving in the right direction.

This book includes 16 chapters and projects that are loosely divided into sections covering lighting for structures and scenes, trackside details, things that go under the rails, switch machines and turnout controls, and operations.

Lighting projects include the use of incandescent bulbs and LEDs, illuminating structures, and installing animated signs. Trackside details include signals, crossing flashers, and working crossing gates. The under-track section provides guidelines for turntables, track scales, and electromagnetic uncouplers.

Turnout controls include control panel design and construction along with wiring guidelines for using accessory decoders as well as toggle and pushbutton control. The operations section includes building a dispatcher's panel as well as adding fast clocks and a telephone system.

Most of these projects involve some level of electronic wiring. Some use off-the-shelf components that only require following simple directions to install them. Others require running and connecting some wires and a few electronic components. The most sophisticated projects may require assembling electronic kits, although many of these are also offered as preassembled units.

Be assured that none of this will be all that difficult, but some familiarity with soldering and working with small electrical components will be a big help. The appendix (page 92) includes a basic primer on soldering, and in my book *Wiring Your Model Railroad,* (Kalmbach) I go into great detail on soldering, wiring, and other basic skills for wiring and electronics projects. I think you'll find it a handy reference for electronics in general as well as for layout (control) wiring.

1 A well-lit building like the Dayton Machine Company, on my friend Dale Martell's HO layout, attracts a lot of attention and adds a sense of drama to a scene.

CHAPTER ONE

Light bulbs, LEDs, and power supplies

Although it might seem out of place to have your layout all lit up in the middle of the day, lights add a lot of realism to structures, streets, and vehicles. One reason lights can add so much to the feeling of reality is that our layout rooms are often dimmer than other areas. This means illuminated scenes draw attention and really come to life, **1**.

2 To provide sufficient power for the lighting needs on my layout I use this 12VDC, 10A power supply.

3 Light bulbs rated at 14-16 VDC, like these from Miniatronics (left) and Model Power, will operate fine at 12 volts and last a lot longer. The Model Power fixture has an adhesive base.

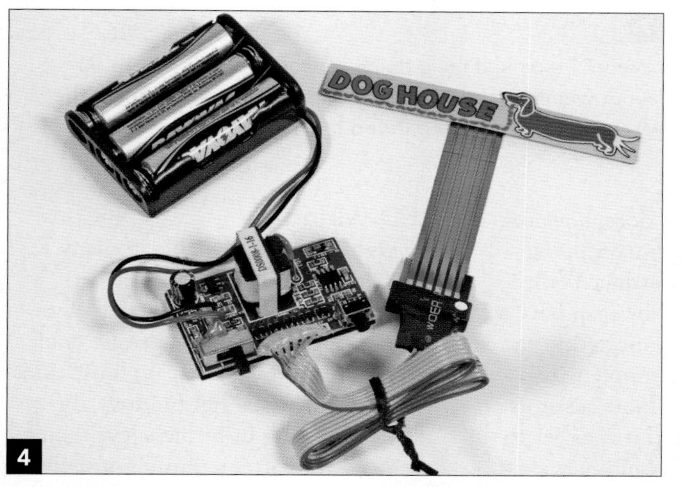

4 Miller Engineering animated display signs operate at 4.5 VDC. They require a specialized power supply; they can also run by three AAA batteries.

5 This buck-booster convertor from All Electronics can convert 5-25 VDC to 0.5-25 VDC, making it possible to connect a lower-voltage power bus off a higher-voltage bus.

In the next three chapters we'll be working with various lighting systems. This chapter provides background on how to select, power, and install incandescent light bulbs and LEDs (light-emitting diodes).

Lights for our layouts require a low-voltage power supply. But what voltage and amperage do you need? Model bulbs are typically rated at about 12-16 volts DC (VDC), although most microbulbs operate at 1.5VDC. LEDs are growing in popularity and they operate at a variety of voltages from 1.5-3.5 VDC at around 20mA. With most bulbs and LEDs requiring only about 20 milliamps (a milliamp, mA, is .001 amp), you can operate a lot of them with a 1A power supply.

Consequently, on a layout you may end up with a mix of different voltage- and amperage-rated bulbs, and there are a couple options for powering them. One option is to buy several plug-in power supplies and scatter them around the layout near your concentration of lights. However, unplugging and plugging them in every time you want to run trains can get tiresome. To avoid this I install a single 12VDC power bus under the layout and connect all my low voltage lights to it. To provide sufficient power I use a 12VDC, 10A unit, **2**. But what about the lights that use less than 12VDC or those that require more?

A bulb rated at 14-16 VDC, **3**, will operate fine at 12VDC. It will also operate cooler and last longer, although not at full brightness. If you have specialized lights requiring an odd voltage, the best option is a separate power supply—as with Miller Engineering animated display signs, **4**, which operate at 4.5VDC.

For lights requiring less than 12 VDC you can easily drop the voltage and current to an acceptable level using resistors or a voltage regulator. Matching the voltage and amperage of power supplies and bulbs is an easy process requiring a little math and the power specifications for the bulb. Ohm's law states that R=e÷I: the resistance (R) required in ohms is equal to the voltage drop required (e), divided by the amperage of the bulb (I).

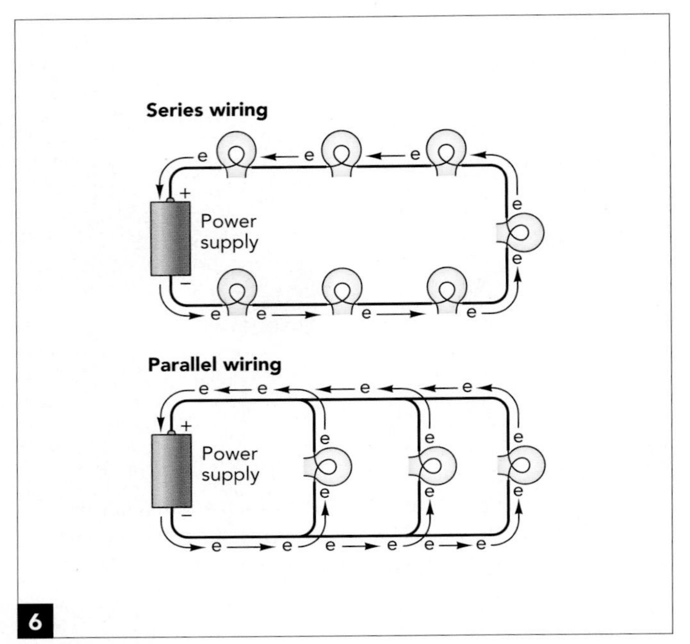

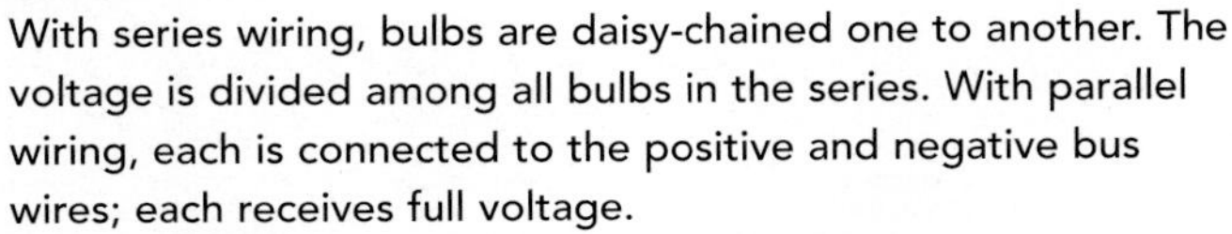

6

With series wiring, bulbs are daisy-chained one to another. The voltage is divided among all bulbs in the series. With parallel wiring, each is connected to the positive and negative bus wires; each receives full voltage.

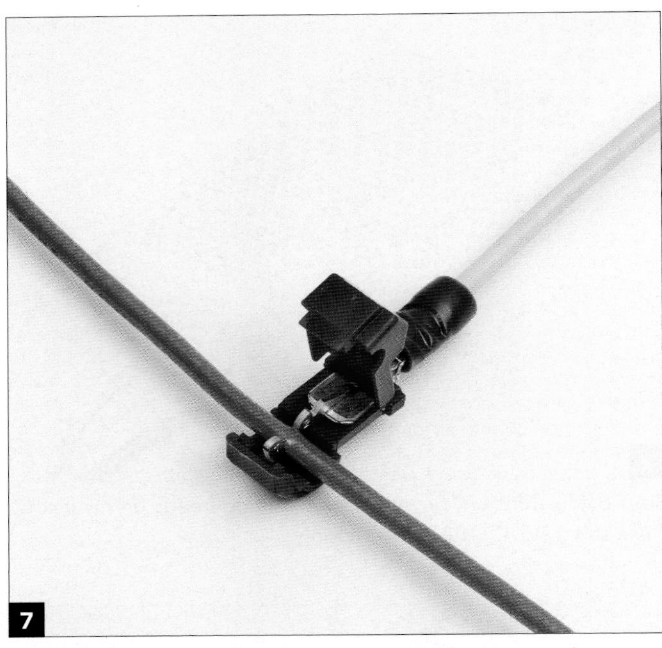

7

I prefer T-taps and male quick connectors for most under-layout wiring. It's easier and quicker than soldering and the wires can be readily separated if necessary.

Thus, if you want to power a 1.5V, 20mA bulb using a 12VDC power supply, the equation is: R=(12-1.5)÷.020, which works out to 525 ohms. Resistors are available in 510- and 560-ohm ratings; it's usually best to use the larger value.

You can also use a voltage regulator circuit which I showed how to build in my book *Wiring Your Model Railroad,* (Kalmbach, 2015) but it is probably cheaper (and much easier) to purchase one from All Electronics or another electronics supplier. They are typically called "buck boost boards" or "step up/step down boards." One common configuration can take 5-25 VDC and put out 0.5-25 VDC at up to 2A, **5**. Simply drop a separate supply wire off the 12VDC power bus, connect it to the step down board, and adjust the voltage setting to create a lower voltage supply for your smaller light bulbs. Just remember to keep the total amperage of the bulbs below the maximum output rating of the circuit board.

When wiring several bulbs they should be connected in parallel, not series. With series wiring the bulbs are basically daisy chained, **6**. The problem with this method is if one bulb burns out it will interrupt the circuit and they all will go out. It does, however, mean you only need one dropping resistor for the entire string. With parallel wiring, the bulbs each have a resistor and each is connected to the positive and negative supply wires. This method requires more resistors but they are cheap and it is easier to trouble-shoot when a bulb burns out since only the one affected goes out. You can eliminate all resistors by using the properly rated sub bus as described in the previous paragraph.

For connecting wires, I prefer insulation-displacement connectors. I especially like T-taps and male quick connectors, **7**, for this since the wires can be easily separated if necessary. Another option is to use terminal strips for multiple connections and interconnect the screws to create a series of negative or positive terminals, **8**. A similar approach is to visit the electrical aisle at your local hardware store and pick up a ground bus bar, **9**. This is a cast-metal strip with screws set in holes along its length. Insert the negative or positive feed wire into one hole and then connect your leads using the other screws. I actually find these easier to use for this purpose than conventional screw terminal blocks.

LED wiring

LEDs are widely available in many sizes and colors. Their prices have dropped considerably in the past few years. Their main advantages are cool operation and long lifespan; limitations include directional light output, difficulty adjusting brightness levels, and the need for current-limiting resistors.

Like bulbs, LEDs are both current- and voltage-dependent. Most operate at about 20mA, but their typical operating voltage ranges from about 1.5VDC for infrared LEDs to 3.5VDC for white versions, while red, green, and yellow LEDs need about 2VDC. The problem is that the output levels of these LEDs vary greatly and you can end up with a brighter light than you really want.

For example, even though a white LED might theoretically only require a 450-ohm resistor, I regularly use a 1000-ohm resistor and the LED is still very bright. My general rule of thumb is to test an LED with a 1000-ohm resistor and then go down in value from there. One option is to use a small potentiometer wired in line with the LED, **10**. Gradually increase the setting and stop when you get to the desired brightness. Without

For multiple connections, interconnect the screws on terminal strips to create a series of negative or positive terminals.

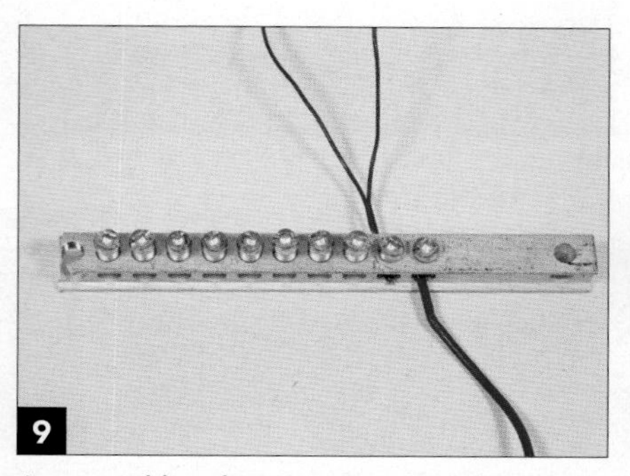

A ground bus bar is a cast metal strip with screws set in holes along its length. It's handy as a terminal strip for many kinds of layout and accessory wiring.

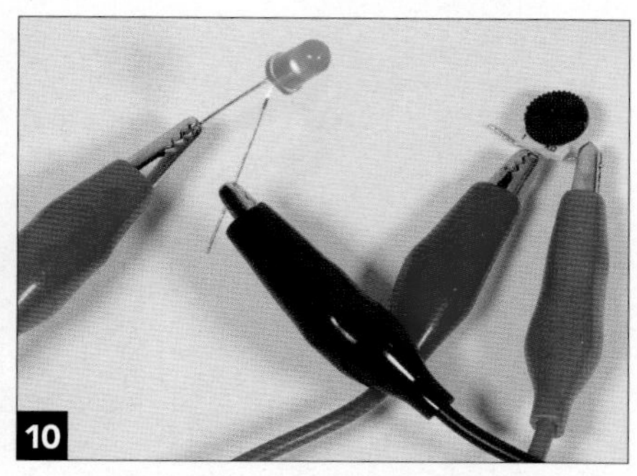

To determine the desired resistor rating, use a 1000-ohm potentiometer wired in line with the LED. Stop at the desired brightness, then measure the resistance across the "pot" with a multimeter.

LED strips offer a quick way to install lighting. They typically come in five-meter-long rolls, but many vendors sell shorter lengths.

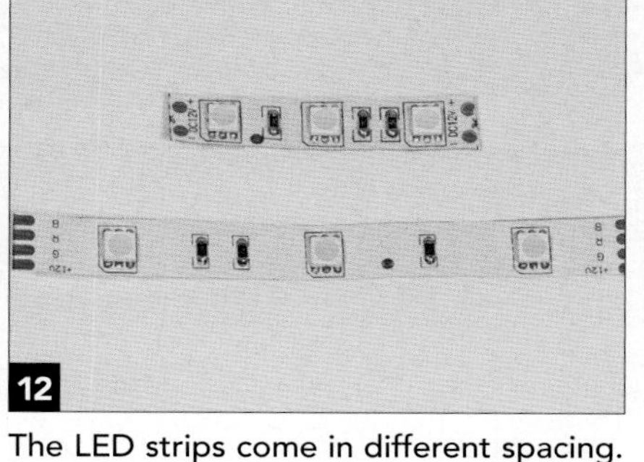

The LED strips come in different spacing. They can be cut into segments of as few as three LEDs, and in most cases they're dimmable.

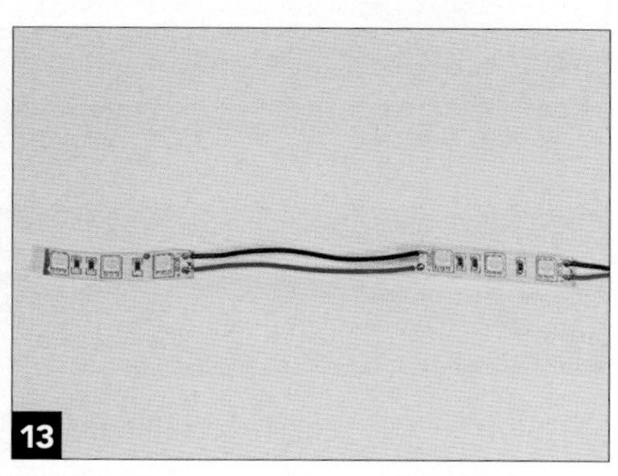

LED segments cut from strips can be wired together for use in large structures or other models.

touching the adjustment knob on the potentiometer, use a multimeter to measure the resistance across the potentiometer leads and that will tell you the size resistor to use.

Another option is LED strips, **11**. I had installed several yards of these under our kitchen cabinets and had several feet left over. They're available from All Electronics, Micro-Mark, and others (also check eBay). They generally come in five-meter rolls but can be purchased in shorter segments. They have from 9 to 18 LEDs per foot, allowing you to spread the light source out or keep them closer together. The really useful aspect is they can be cut into three-LED segments, **12**, and wired together, **13**. Most are also dimmable. Be warned that they can only be cut at the points marked on the strips—cut them elsewhere and they will not work.

Each small surface mount device (SMD) LED on the strip also has an SMD resistor wired with it, and the segments can be powered with a 12VDC power supply. Since they typically have an adhesive backing they can be easily installed in many places, such as inside a structure or under a bridge. Although it's possible to use them for layout lighting, be aware that they typically require about 1 amp per meter, so you could easily overwhelm your existing power supply.

There are also individual miniature SMD LEDs, **14**, which can be used as miniature light bulbs. In Chapter 3 we'll be looking at a lighting system that uses these; you can also make your own if you have a steady hand and are good at soldering. One good source for these is Ngineering.com. I have used SMD LEDs for locomotive headlights and they are also useful for lighting structures, streets, yards, and other scenes.

With these small SMD LEDs I typically use a ½-watt SMD resistor. This probably is a bit more than necessary, but the ½W resistor will

Miniature surface-mount LEDs are tiny. One (above left) is shown with a resistor (above right) and circuit board (bottom). These are from Ngineering.com.

operate cooler and last a lot longer than a ¼W resistor. Ngineering also sells small circuit boards for mounting these tiny resistors and LEDs, which makes it easier to solder wire leads between a power supply and the SMD LED.

Now that you have a grasp of the basics of light bulbs and LEDs, let's move on to Chapter 2 and look at some ways to use light bulbs and LEDs in structures.

CHAPTER TWO

Lighting small structures

Interior lighting, along with a few detail items or a photo print, gives model structures life and makes them appear occupied. Scenery applied up to the structure base prevents light leaks at the bottom.

One of the most difficult aspects of modeling structures is lighting the interiors so they look realistic, **1**. It's easy to end up with too little or too much light, with hot spots where light is visible through the walls of a structure, or with undecorated areas showing through windows. Let's look at some ways to handle these issues.

2

A quick way to check for hot spots and light leaks is to insert a small flashlight or bare bulb into the structure.

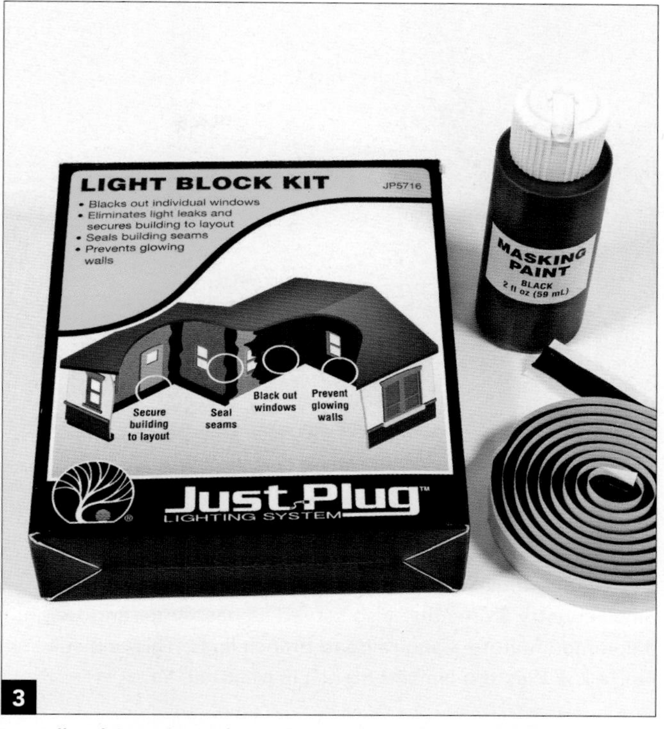

3

Woodland Scenics makes a light block kit that contains black paint and caulking putty.

For any structure molded in plastic you need to deal with the potential for hot spots. One quick way to check is to place a small flashlight or bare bulb inside the structure and examine the exterior, **2**. You'll usually see many areas of glowing plastic where the light bleeds through—not the realistic appearance we're looking for. Painting the exterior helps (and will also provide a better appearance than plastic, even the "molded in realistic color" variety), but you can still have trouble areas, especially with light-color buildings.

I usually begin by giving the inside of the structure a coat of dark opaque paint such as black or brown—this will help prevent light bleed through. I usually just spray-paint the inner walls before assembly. It's easier to get a good coat of paint on the inside *before* gluing the walls together. To keep the corner edges clean for gluing, I apply strips of blue painter's tape. If the structure is already built you can carefully brush-paint the inside.

For light leaks at joints, you can run a bead of black caulk where needed. Woodland Scenics makes a light block kit that contains black paint and caulking putty designed specifically for this task, **3**. You also need to check for cracks around windows and doors as light may escape there too. As you assemble kits, keep the roof in mind since light can escape there too. On some buildings I like to make the roof removable in case I ever need to replace a bulb or LED, or if I decide to add more interior details. In most cases, pieces of stripwood or styrene glued to the inner edges of the structure or roof will provide support and help block light from escaping.

Next decide what kind of lights you want to install and where to put them. Keep in mind that it is often better to install several small lights instead of one large one. Several small bulbs or LEDs at lower intensity will light the inside of a structure more evenly than a single bulb burning at full power. Multiple lights are also less likely to result in hot spots. You can use a potentiometer or resistor to reduce the intensity of a light as described in Chapter 1.

Lighting a store

Let's take a look at how I added lighting to a small wooden grocery store and flagstop station. I chose this kit because it's very similar to one near my childhood home in Maxwell, Va., that still sits next to the old N&W Norton Branch line, **4**. This laser-cut wood kit was produced by Kingmill Enterprises. Although it's no longer available, the lighting techniques are the same as with many other small structures. Because the structure is wood I wasn't concerned with hot spots and didn't bother with painting the inside walls.

Whenever you light a structure interior, you need to avoid the "empty" look. One option is to make the windows translucent so viewers can see that lights are on but cannot see the empty room. This can be done by sanding the inside surface of clear plastic glazing with very fine sandpaper or spraying the glazing with clear flat finish (such as Dullcote).

The opaque black paint in the Woodland Scenics light block kit can be used for painting the inside of windows that don't need to be illuminated. The company also offers a translucent window film that is applied behind the windows to give the building the appearance it is occupied without requiring furnishings, **5**.

Small country stores that also served as passenger and freight depots were once a common feature along railroad branch lines. This one still stands next to the old Norfolk & Western Norton Branch in Maxwell, Va.

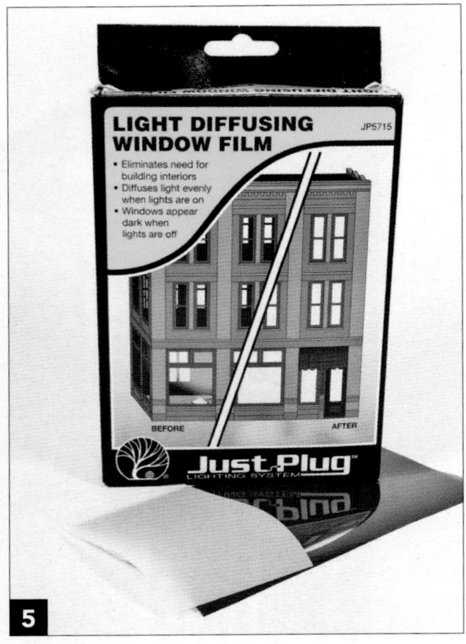

Frosted glazing, such as Woodland Scenics translucent window film, can help give structures the appearance of being occupied without requiring furnishings.

A check for light leaks in this wood structure revealed some gaps around each window and door.

Even though in this case I was not concerned with hot spots, I did check for light leaking through cracks around the windows and doors. You can easily see the light leaks around each window and door in photo **6**.

To remedy this I used a bit of the Woodland Scenics light blocking caulk around the inside of all of these cracks, **7**. A bead of gap-filling cyanoacrylate adhesive (CA) with a coat of black paint will provide a similar result. The net result was elimination of the light leaks, **8**.

Interior details

A step up from frosted window glazing is adding interior detail or artwork and photos to represent an interior. For this store I considered several options. One approach was to do a Google image search for "old country store interior photos"—this resulted in some worthwhile images. You can print these on a color printer, attach them to cardstock backing, and install them in a building. These can be glued directly to the walls. Another trick is to bend the cardstock to create a "room" or shadowbox and glue that in place. If the building will not be near the edge of the layout you can always just fit a sheet of black construction paper inside to hide the bare walls and prevent the see-through effect, **9**.

For a fully furnished look, City Classics offers printed photos of a variety of interiors. These are printed on translucent white film designed to be backlit for a more realistic and diffused light effect. I gave the City Classics product a try, deciding that the no. 1304 hardware store print closely

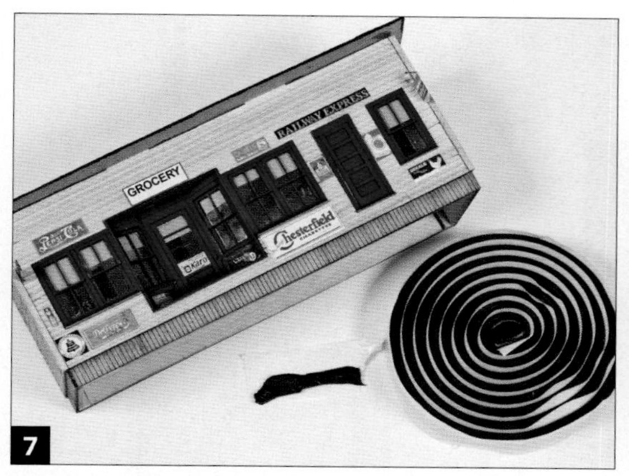

The Woodland Scenics light-blocking caulk works well to seal cracks.

Eliminating the light leaks greatly improves the realism and overall appearance.

A piece of black construction paper is an effective view block, preventing a see-through effect.

City Classics' no. 1304 hardware store interior looked like a good representation of a small county store.

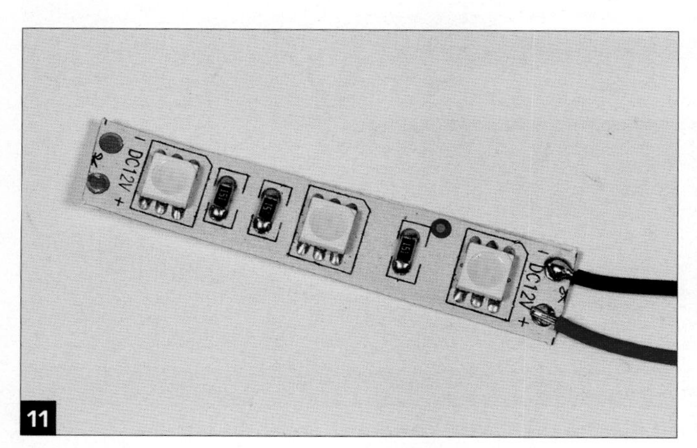

I cut a section from an LED strip light and soldered red and black wires to the contacts.

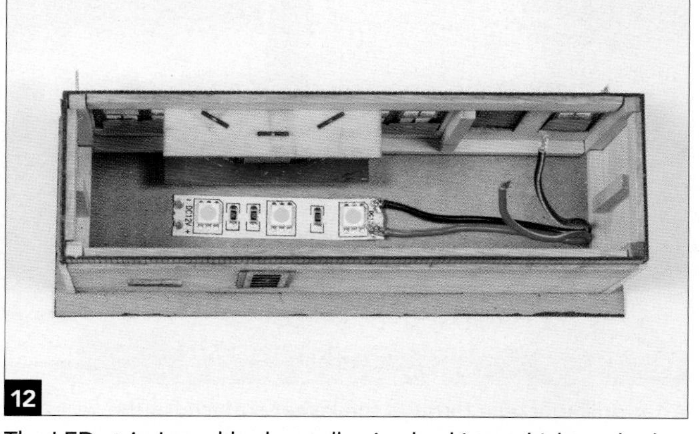

The LED strip I used had an adhesive backing, which worked well for securing it to the interior ceiling.

resembled the inside of a small country store, **10**.

Before installing the City Classics interior, I installed the lights. Since this is a small structure, I opted for what has become my favorite method, LED strips. I cut a three-LED section and soldered red and black wires to the positive and negative contacts, **11**. Using the 3M adhesive backing I attached it to the inside ceiling, **12**.

With the light source installed, it was time to add the "furnishings." Following the instructions I glued the print behind the front windows using Testor's Clear Parts Cement, **13**. The film was such a good fit to the roof and bottom of the structure that the

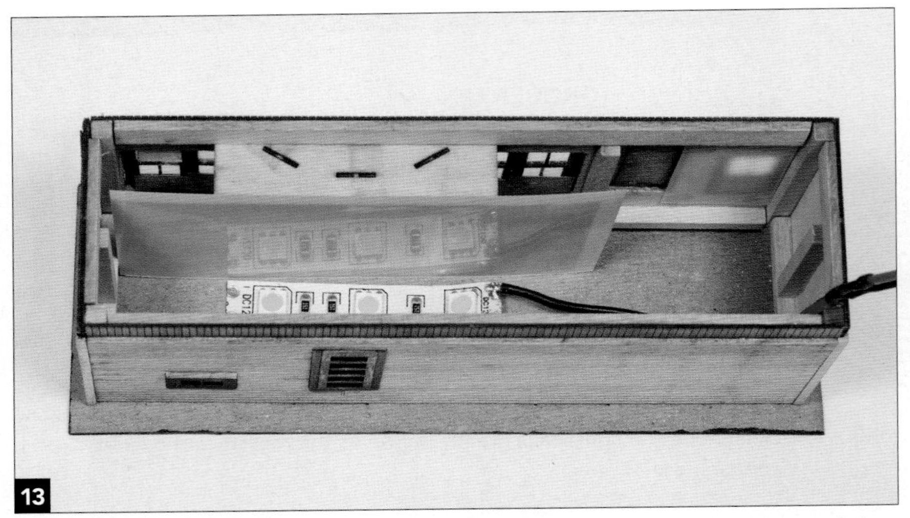

13

The City Classics film with the image on it can be bent in a shallow curve around the inside of the front or simply glued to the interior frame behind the windows and door as shown here.

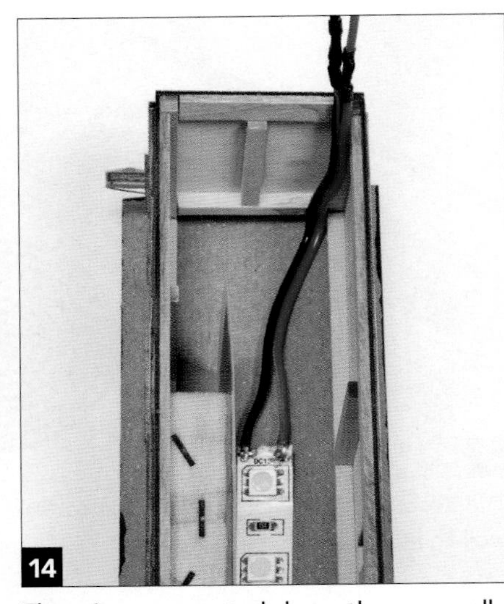

14

The wires are routed down the rear wall. I tacked them in place with CA.

15

After drilling a hole through the layout surface for the wires, I routed them to the 12VDC power bus under the layout.

cardstock provided in the kit was not necessary.

Once the glue dried I routed the wires down the rear wall and tacked them in place with CA, **14**. After attaching a 12VDC power supply it was apparent that the LEDs needed dimming. Using a small potentiometer as described in Chapter 8, I adjusted the brightness of the lighting and soldered a 220-ohm resistor to the negative wire.

For the final installation I drilled a hole in the layout where the back corner would be located, fed the wires to to my power bus, **15**, and connected them using T-taps and male quick connects. A scattering of scenery around the base of the structure blended it in and prevented light leaking out the bottom, **1**. The completed structure takes me back a few years to the well-stocked candy counter in the Maxwell country store.

CHAPTER THREE

Lighting a large structure

In the last two chapters I've explained how to cobble together lights, resistors, wires, and power supplies to light up your buildings. In this chapter we'll take a look at adapting the Woodland Scenics modular system to illuminate a large structure and surrounding area, **1**.

The crew is hard at work moving recently unloaded freight from the loading dock into the freight house. The combination of interior lights, softly lit windows, illuminated freight area, and building exterior lights makes this an eye-catching scene.

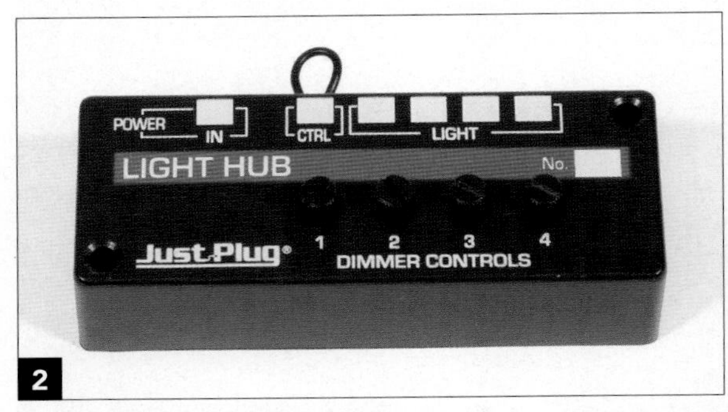

2

Light Hubs are the heart of the Just Plug system, serving as connection and control points for light accessories.

3

The 16VAC, 1A power supply can operate about 50 of the Just Plug lights.

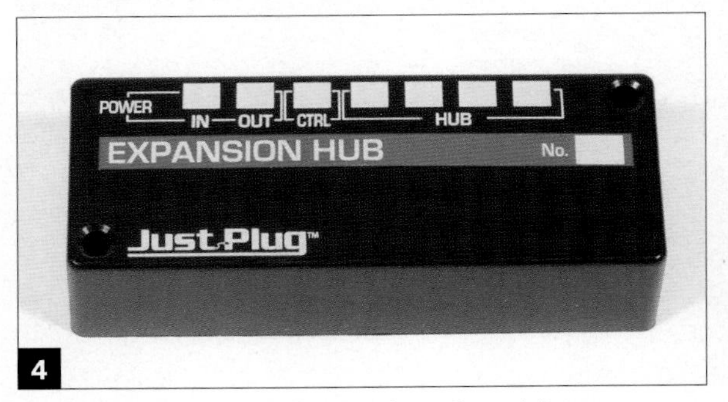

4

Expansion Hubs have four sockets for adding more Light Hubs. They can be daisy-chained until you reach the capacity of the power supply.

5

Expansion cables as well as an on/off switch are also available.

The Woodland Scenics Just Plug system features an array of lights, power supplies, controllers, and pre-wired plugs and cables. Although more expensive than using individual LEDs, bulbs, and other components, the Just Plug components are handy, easy to install, and work well. They are based on small high-intensity LEDs which require very little current, meaning a single power supply can operate dozens of them. Let's take a look at the various components, what they do, and how they are connected, then we'll walk through some basic installations.

The heart of the Just Plug system is the Light Hub, **2**. Each Light Hub has four sockets where LED lights can be plugged in and a built-in potentiometer to control the intensity of the LED brightness at each socket. (A tip: Do not force the dimmer control knob past the point where you feel resistance, as you can permanently damage the potentiometer.) A 16VAC power supply, **3**, is available, or you can use the 16VAC terminals on a power pack. Inside the Light Hub is a bridge rectifier, capacitor, resistors, and transistors which convert the 16VAC to DC power.

If you need more sockets than available on one Light Hub, you will need an Expansion Hub, **4**. Various expansion cables are also available as well as an on/off switch, **5**, to control the main Expansion Hub or individual Light Hubs. Up to four Light Hubs can then be plugged into each Expansion Hub, and additional Expansion Hubs can be daisy-chained up to the limit of the power supply, **6**. The hubs come with a double-sided foam tape backing as well as wood screws for mounting them on either the fascia or under the layout.

Another power and control option for DCC users is the Illuminator from NCE, **7**. This small accessory decoder has ports for plugging in up to three Just Plug lights, and it offers up to 15 special effects for each port.

Considering that the various lights available for use with the system are each rated at about 20 to 30mA, a 1A power supply can power about 50 of them. Lights include individual LEDs with self-stick backing that can be used inside structures (or in many other applications) and a variety of streetlights, gooseneck lights, and other fixtures, **8**. Automobiles with headlights and taillights and a police car with a flashing "cherry" on top are also part of the system, **9**.

Some of the lights come with an attached plug. However, most have wires about 36" long with bare ends that are inserted in a pinch clamp ("Linking Plug") that then plugs into the socket. Typically two or three light fixtures are wired into these. The current demand of the various combinations of lights connected to Linking Plugs ranges from 20-30mA and should be limited to just those lights supplied with each Linking Plug.

Installation

I used a variety of Just Plug lights and components in a new section of my HO Piedmont Southern layout. To represent the Southern Railway freight terminal and office at Charlottesville, I chose a Walthers Water Street Freight Terminal kit. The kit is molded in a reddish brown styrene designed to complement the brick exterior. I painted the building's exterior with a variety of red brick colors.

With the structure assembled, I used a small flashlight to check for light leaks, **10**, and added black caulk from the Woodland Scenics light block kit where needed, **11**. Roof joints in particular can be problem areas. This caulk is very sticky, so moisten your fingertips a little to make it easier to work with. I also added strips of styrene under each end of the roof to help block light leaks.

Due to the size of this structure I decided not to furnish each office. Instead I cut and applied Woodland Scenics light-diffusing window film behind the windows in the office portion, **12**. A roll of window tint film is also part of the kit. It makes the rooms behind the film appear dark when the interior lights are off. If the light-diffusing film is used alone, the windows just have a frosted white appearance, which is what I did.

The kit includes a roll of adhesive micro-dots to attach the film, **13**. To

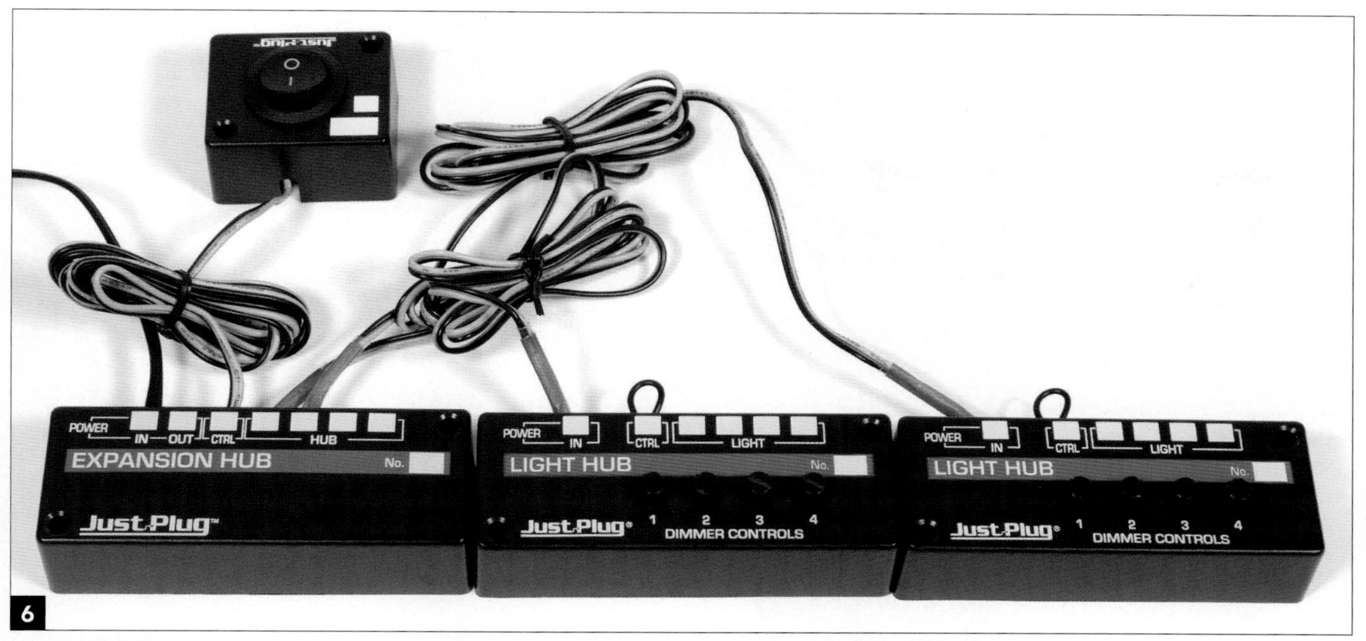

This combination of one Expansion Hub and two Light Hubs can power and control up to eight fixtures (more with some light combinations).

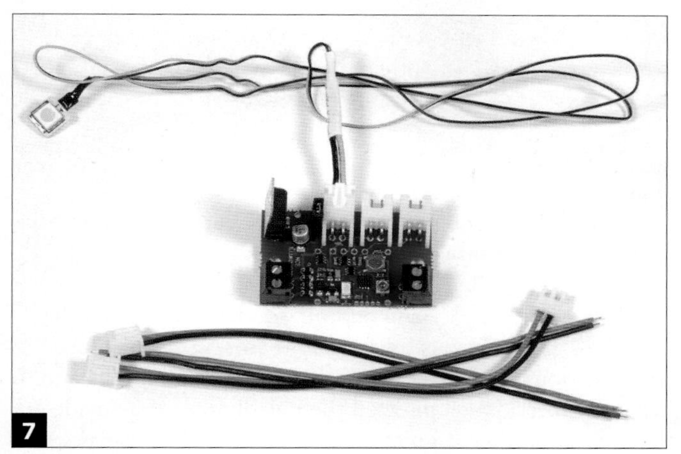

NCE offers a Digital Command Control (DCC) accessory decoder called the Illuminator which can control up to three Just Plug lights.

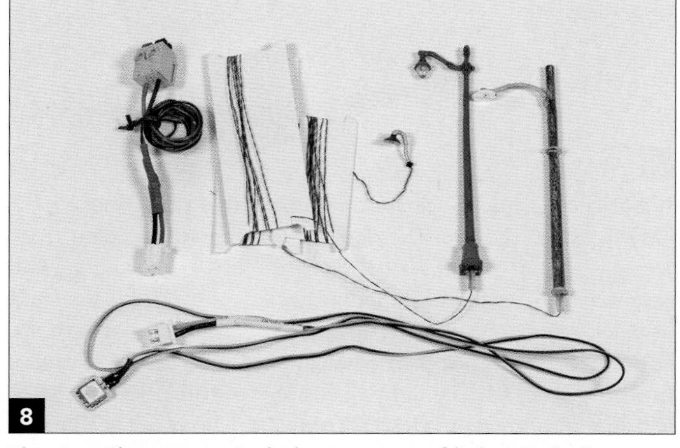

The Just Plug system includes a variety of lights, including individual LEDs and streetlights. The small wires are inserted into the Linking Plug (far left) to connect to a Light Hub.

A variety of automobiles with headlights and taillights including a police car with flashing red light are part of the Just Plug system. Accessories are available in HO, N, and O scales.

A flashlight revealed a few light leaks in the injection-molded Walthers building, including one in the roof joint.

11
Strips of black caulk from the Woodland Scenics light block kit sealed the roof joint.

12
I cut and applied rectangles of light-diffusing window film to the interiors of both walls visible from the aisle.

13
Adhesive micro-dots—circles of double-sided tape—make it easy to attach the film. The dots are less messy than glue.

14
I applied a sheet of black construction paper to the entire back wall using the adhesive dots.

save material I simply applied a sheet of black construction paper to the entire back wall since it faced away from the aisle, **14**. The light-diffusing window film prevents viewers from seeing the inside of the structure and the black paper while evenly lighting up the front and aisle side windows.

Now let's move to the freight house portion of the building. I wanted the roll-up doors on the loading dock open but didn't want to deal with lighting and decorating the entire interior. Taking a tip from Jeff Wilson's book *50 Ways to a Better-Looking Layout*, (Kalmbach, 2013) to cut things down to size I built a shadowbox of .060" styrene sheet only a couple inches deep, running the entire length of the inside of the structure. I painted the interior walls of the shadowbox black and the floor gray, then installed it behind the loading dock, **15**. A few strips of styrene attached to the inside wall provided a stable attachment point.

To fill the shadowbox interior I used photos of stacks of boxes glued to the back walls as well as various other details, **16**. Lighting the interior was fairly simple. Using their adhesive backing, I installed two of the stick-on LED lights to the roof of each section of the building, **17**. The potentiometers on the Light Hubs make it easy to adjust the brightness.

Exterior lighting

I installed a gooseneck lamp over each loading dock door and one over the main entry, **18**. To give train crews some light for spotting and unloading cars I added pole-mounted lights along the tracks. The wooden pole lights come with extensions that plug into the bottom of each, which I used for mounting the lights. Here's how:

Because my layout consists of ½" foam insulation sheet over ½" plywood, I needed a way to stabilize the pole lights. I drilled 5⁄32" holes through the foam and plywood, then inserted the extensions in them. Next I threaded the wires through the extensions and inserted the pole lights—they made great plug-in sockets, **19**. If the poles lean a bit, just insert some small shims cut from toothpicks alongside the buried extensions.

I drilled holes beneath each section of the building and fed all the wires down to the Light Hubs, **20**—the ribbon cable powers a sign I'll install in the next chapter.

The Just Plug system made it easy to add lights to this structure and its surroundings. The real advantage is the ability to adjust the brightness of each light and to install all the lights without needing a soldering iron. Future projects for me include lighting a passenger station, parking lot, and passenger platforms, as well as an industrial area. I'm sure you have plenty of ideas of how to add these lights to your structures and scenes.

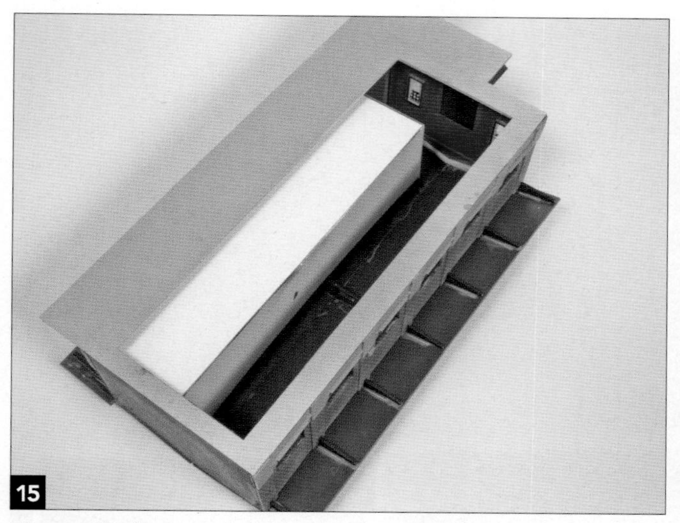

15 The shadowbox, made from .060" styrene sheet, extends for the entire length of the freight house.

16 To prevent that empty look I glued photos of stacks of boxes (courtesy of Jeff Wilson) to the back walls of the shadowbox.

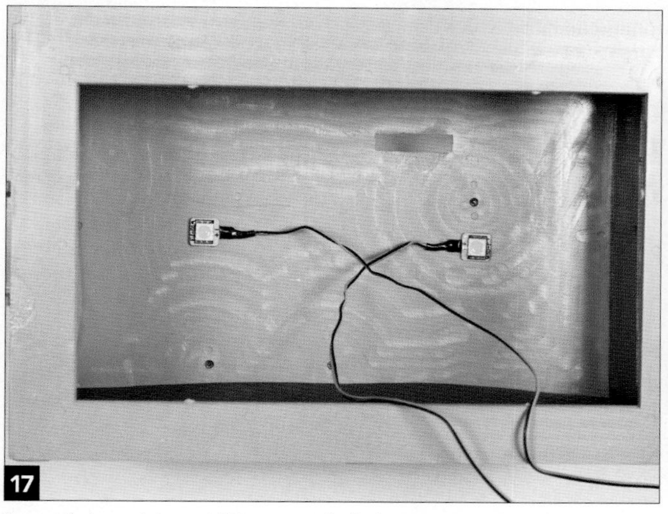

17 Two of the stick-on LEDs provide lighting in each section of the building.

18 A gooseneck lamp over the main entry door and each of the loading dock doors add to the scene.

19 I inserted the extensions supplied with the light poles into holes drilled in the top of the layout, then used them as plug-in sockets for mounting the poles.

20 Holes drilled through the layout base allow wires to pass through to Light Hubs under the layout.

CHAPTER FOUR

Animated neon signs

Miller Engineering offers a variety of simulated neon and other illuminated signs. They can be free-standing or mounted to structures or backdrops. Many are based on prototype signs, such as the H&C sign (inset). *Inset photo by Mike Whye/Visit Virginia's Blue Ridge*

Each era has certain features that immediately convey a sense of time and place. Neon signs in particular were extremely popular in the United States from the 1920s through the 1960s. Animated neon signs of the 1950s are especially evocative of the transition era when steam was giving way to streamlined diesels. These brightly colored, nostalgic additions to city skylines help create the mood of that era.

2 Each circuit board is attached to a battery pack that holds three AAA batteries. Boards have on/off and animation-selection switches.

3 Mounting the circuit board on a piece of soft foam practically eliminates the high-frequency sound generated by the circuit.

4 Be aware of unrealistic shadows on the sky if you mount a sign too close to a sky backdrop.

5 Installing the sign in front of another building makes shadows logical and less noticeable.

Miller Engineering produces a variety of animated, illuminated signs that mimic these neon advertising signs of the 1950s. Some, like the Dr. Pepper, H&C Coffee, and Sauer's Vanilla signs are based on actual signs that still exist, **1**. Others are fictional, but based on popular advertising signs from the period. For my layout I have chosen signs which I have either seen or have a personal connection to. For example, the Mr. Peanut sign atop the freight house in Chapter 3 is a reminder of all the trips I made as a child to the Planters Peanuts store on East Broad Street in Richmond, Va. I also remember the Sauer's sign in Richmond as well as the Dr Pepper and H&C Coffee signs in Roanoke.

The Miller signs consist of flexible electroluminescent sheets with the advertising image printed on them. They are designed so that several areas of the sheet light up, illuminating different sections of the sign in a number of sequences creating the animated effect.

A circuit board connected to the sign via a strip of ribbon cable controls the sequence of the lights. The small circuit boards for each are the same. Each circuit board is attached to a battery pack that holds three AAA batteries, **2**, which provide the 4.5VDC to power the signs. Miller also sells a 4.5V transformer as an option.

The circuit boards are programmed with 46 different lighting sequences or chase patterns. There is a small pushbutton on the board that allows you to advance through all of them and see how each pattern will look with your specific sign. Do this before installation, as it can be difficult to do later. Make sure you advance through the patterns slow enough for them to successfully load into memory. There's also an on/off slide switch on the edge of the circuit board.

These boards emit a low-volume, high-pitch tone that some find annoying. I've found that mounting the circuit board on a piece of spongy foam practically eliminates this, **3**.

Mount a printout or photo of a building to black Gator board with spray adhesive such as 3M Super 77.

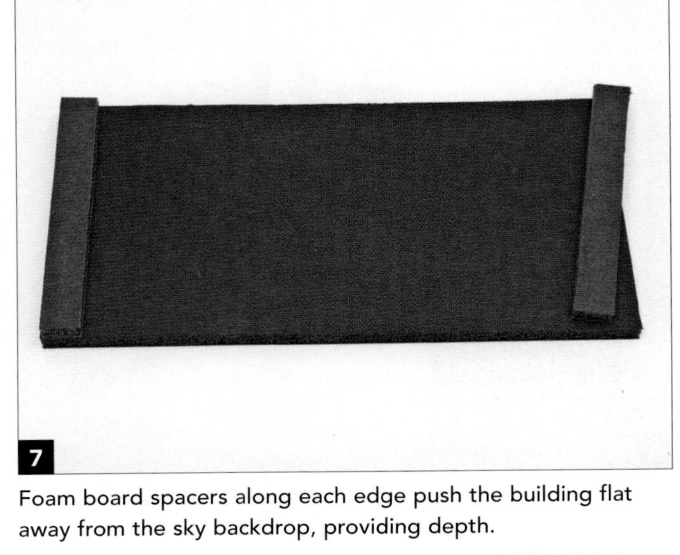

Foam board spacers along each edge push the building flat away from the sky backdrop, providing depth.

This background photo was glued directly to the sky backdrop to provide a background for the illuminated sign. Note the circles of hook-and-loop fasteners at left.

A thin slot cut in the layout base allows feeding the connector and ribbon cable from the under-table-mounted circuit board to the sign.

Location and installation

The signs can be attached directly to a building, or you can use a supporting structure designed to make them free-standing. I especially like using these signs with photo flats mounted on pieces of foam board where they can help make a narrow space look like a large city.

If you're placing one in the background near a backdrop, be aware of potential shadows, **4**. A shadow on a sky backdrop ruins the overall effect. For these installations, keep signs in front of other buildings or in front of a photo of a building where a shadow would be logical, **5**.

The ribbon cable connecting the circuit board to the sign is about a foot long. Extension cables aren't practical, as the long signal path can cause signs to malfunction. Thus if you plan on installing one in a building, make sure it's accessible in case you need to reset the circuit, change the chase pattern, replace batteries, or turn it on and off. For a couple of installations on my layout the ribbon cable was too short to reach under the layout. For these I had to install the controllers behind the backdrop. If possible, though, I run the ribbon cable down through a slot cut in the scenery base and mount the controller under the layout.

Let's look at different ways to mount these signs. To install one on a photo against the backdrop, I start by cutting out the photo to be used. With spray adhesive such as 3M Super 77, I mount the photo on a piece of black Gator board, **6**. The foam in gator board is sandwiched by a laminate material (instead of the paper used on foam core), so the material is temperature and moisture stable and won't warp. To get the depth necessary for mounting the signs, I add strips of foam board along the edges on each side. These can either be built up in layers or you can purchase thicker material for this purpose, **7**.

The connector and ribbon cable can be attached directly to the back of the foam board.

With the sign installed, add the batteries or power supply and flip the power switch on the circuit board.

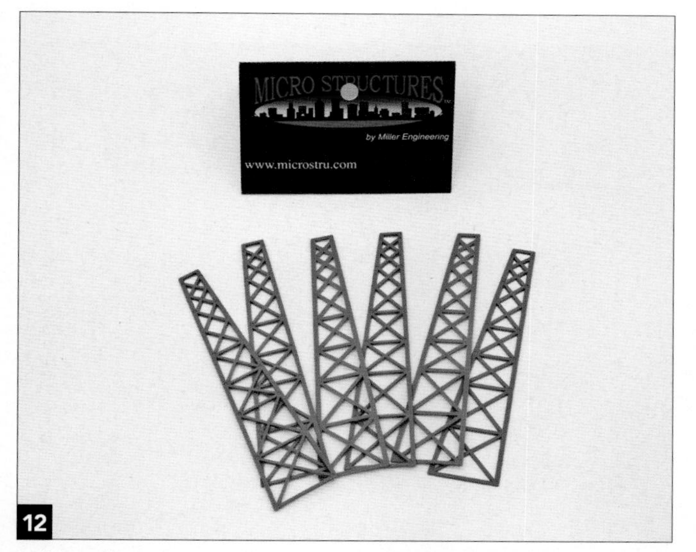

Miller sells a plastic support kit (no. 990) of girders that can be glued to the backs of signs. This turns them into free-standing billboards.

The girders can be cut to any height needed. Use a razor saw and miter box to ensure a square cut.

Next I attach photo backdrops directly to the sky backdrop or wall where the building with the sign will be placed, **8**. To avoid the shadow effect, it's often best to apply two layers of photo prints. With the background building installed, I attach small hook-and-loop tabs (such as Velcro) to the back of the flat with the sign. Finally I press the flat against the backdrop so the hook-and-loop tabs hold it in place but allow it to be removable. This layered effect adds to the feeling of depth and provides the space needed for the connector and ribbon cable. Wrapping the photo of the building around the edge helps disguise the black foam spacer—necessary in some locations.

Cut a slot ¾" long and ¼" wide in the top of the layout directly below the location of the sign and feed the connector and ribbon cable from the circuit board up through it, **9**. If there's room, the circuit board can be placed behind the backdrop but that can present problems if you need to easily get to it later.

I place the circuit board on a piece of soft foam and mount it on a shelf or support joist under the layout. The connector and ribbon cable can then be fed up and attached directly to the back of the foam board, **10**. Although epoxy or hot glue is recommended for attaching the connector, I've found that double-sided foam tape works well, and if necessary is easier to remove should you decide to move a sign later. With the sign installed, pop in the batteries and flip the power switch on the circuit board, **11**.

If you want a free-standing sign, Miller sells a plastic billboard structure (no. 990) that can be glued to the back of the sign using CA, **12**. These work well for installing the signs on the roofs of full-sized buildings. The plastic castings can be cut to fit the various signs available and can be painted with common hobby paints. Test-fit the

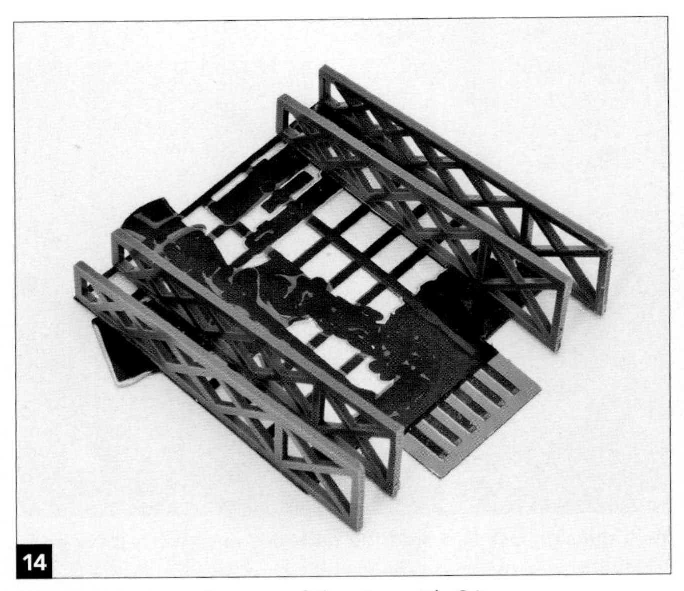

Glue supports to the rear of the sign with CA.

I glued the Planters sign to the roof of the freight house.

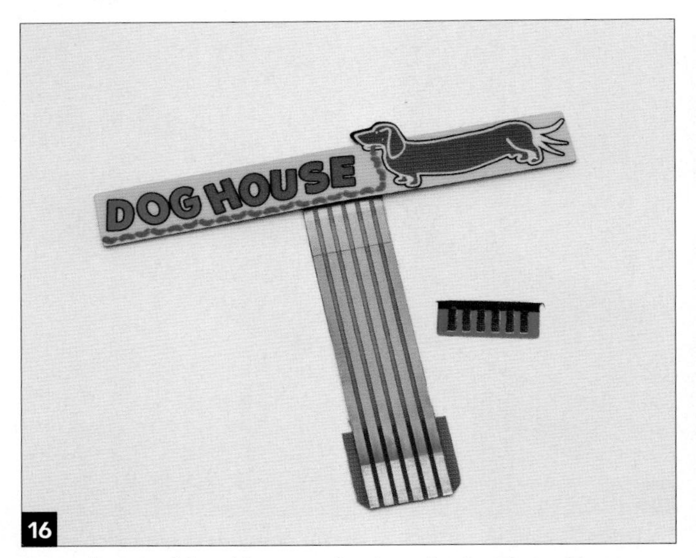

Signs designed for side mounting have both side and bottom connector strips. The unused connector should be cut off.

I installed a terminal strip, with the power supply wires attached, under my layout and connected the circuit board wires to it.

billboard supports against the back of the sign and decide what length you want them. Use a razor saw to cut the castings at a horizontal cross member, **13**, making sure the cuts are square.

Paint the supports before gluing them to the sign. Attach several strips of double-sided tape to a piece of cardboard, place the flat side of the support that will be glued to the sign on the tape, and spray-paint the supports (I used black). Glue the supports to the sign using CA, **14**, making sure the bases for each are even with each other. I used four supports for the Planters Peanuts sign. I cut a slot in the roof of the freight house building (from Chapter 10) for the ribbon cable and connector and attached it to the sign. I then glued the sign in its final location, **15**. It's shown in its finished state in **3-1**.

Miller Engineering also offers versions that represent side-mounted signs. These have both a connector strip along the bottom of the sign and a short section of ribbon cable with a connector strip on its end. Once you decide which mounting method you will use, the other connector should be cut off, **16**. To mount the sign on the side of a building a slit is cut through the building wall and the ribbon cable is inserted through it and connected to the longer ribbon cable inside.

You can use either the AAA battery pack or a transformer to power the circuit boards. Since I had a regulated 4.5VDC power supply, I decided to use it. Each circuit board uses 95mA (.095 amps), so a 1A power supply can easily power 10 of them. I installed a terminal strip under my layout and simply connected the circuit board wires to it, **17**. Keep in mind that the red wires are positive and black are negative when you connect the circuit board to an external power supply.

CHAPTER FIVE

Crossbucks and flashing signals

Railroads have always had a responsibility to protect highway, road, and street crossings to prevent accidents. Well into the 1900s this often meant having a crossing guard who would wave a red flag or hold a stop sign as trains approached. By the 1930s and '40s, automatically controlled red flashing lights and bells were becoming more common to warn of oncoming trains, **1**.

Flashing lights add a nice animation to a grade-crossing scene, and they're easy to add without having to deal with track circuits.

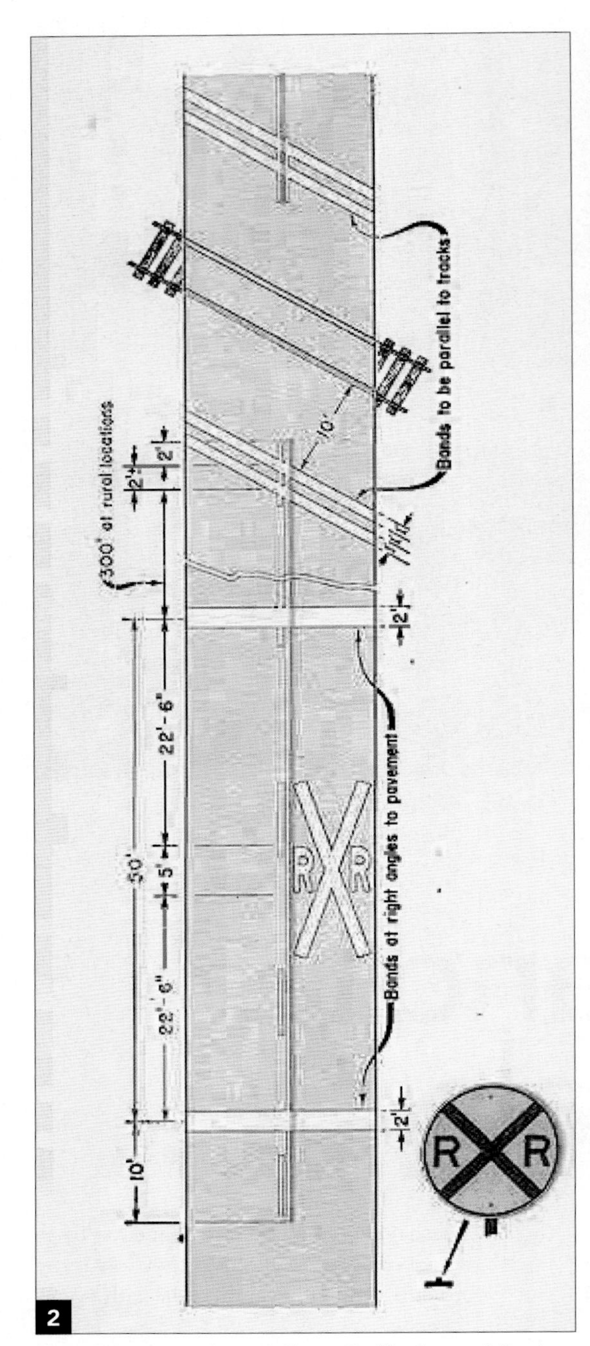

2 The 1948 *Manual on Uniform Traffic Control Devices* provided guidance on pavement markings.

3 Summit Customcuts offers road marking decals, including the extended RR "X" in both N and HO scales.

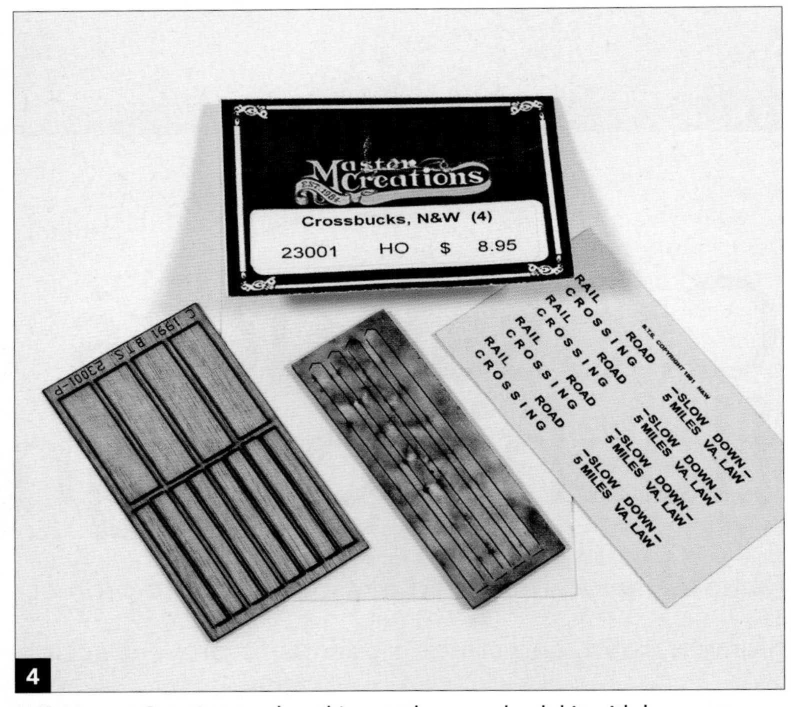

4 BTS Master Creations makes this wooden crossbuck kit with laser-cut parts and decals.

Typically signals and bells are only used at moderate to heavily traveled grade crossings. In rural areas, especially on branch and secondary lines, you still often find only crossbucks and warning signs. This provides modelers a wide variety of choices when modeling grade crossings. But what goes where?

According to the 1948 *Manual on Uniform Traffic Control Devices* (MUTCD), which covers the period I model, a 30" diameter yellow with black lettering railroad warning sign must be placed 300-500 feet in advance of a railroad crossing in rural areas, and 100 feet or less in residential or business areas. The shorter distances were also allowed for special circumstances such as curves or other conditions that limited visibility. (Copies of various MUTCD editions from 1935-2009 are available at ceprofs.civil.tamu.edu/ghawkins/MUTCD-History.htm).

Crossbucks were to be placed on the right-hand side of the roadway, 10-15 feet from the center of the nearest track and not less than 6 feet from the pavement. Crossbucks were to be white with black lettering with the center of the crossbuck 10 feet above the pavement. Signage included notification of the number of tracks in the crossing. Other details of post color and additional markings were left to the railroads and state requirements.

The MUTCD also provided guidance on pavement markings for crossings, **2**. Note in particular the double white lines 10 feet back from the tracks and the 2-foot-wide white line adjacent to the crossing gate or crossbuck. I have seen photos with various combinations of these markings—often the double white lines are not present and only the wide single line was used. I use Woodland Scenics road marker pens for adding these details as well as the double yellow lines down the center of the road. Summit Customcuts (www.summit-customcuts.com) offers decals (RSD-002), including the extended RR "X" road markings in both N and HO scales, **3**.

The main impediment to modeling grade crossings is the cost. Crossbucks and warning signs are inexpensive options, and depending on prototypical accuracy can run anywhere from a few dollars for plastic models to $15 for brass kits. An installation with a pair of warning lights and bells can exceed $150. I'll show you how I did a simple rural road crossing with only the crossbucks, then another crossing with flashing lights.

Crossbucks

During the 1950s (and even today) many rural road crossings had just the yellow warning sign and a wooden crossbuck. Crossbucks and signs are available in a number of kits and cast plastic versions. BTS Master Creations makes a wooden kit (23001) with laser-cut parts and decals, **4**, correct for my era and the state of Virginia where my HO scale Piedmont Southern is located. Since the road crossing I modeled was short and perpendicular to the tracks, there was no place for a warning sign, limiting this project to a pair of crossbucks on each side of the tracks. Since it is a dirt road there are no pavement markings involved.

The BTS kit is easy, requiring only a couple hours. After punching out the crossbuck arms and sign boards I painted them white, and while they dried I painted the posts dark brown. This mimics creosote-soaked posts. To speed drying I hit the acrylic paint

Railroads have installed automatic flashers at grade crossings since the early 1900s. This one warns Virginia residents to slow to the legal speed limit. *Harold Reid*

I glued the painted crossarms and sign boards to the posts using super glue.

The decals reminding motorists of Virginia's 5-mph speed limit help set a place and time on the layout.

An old Model T pickup waits obligingly at the crossing for a passing train.

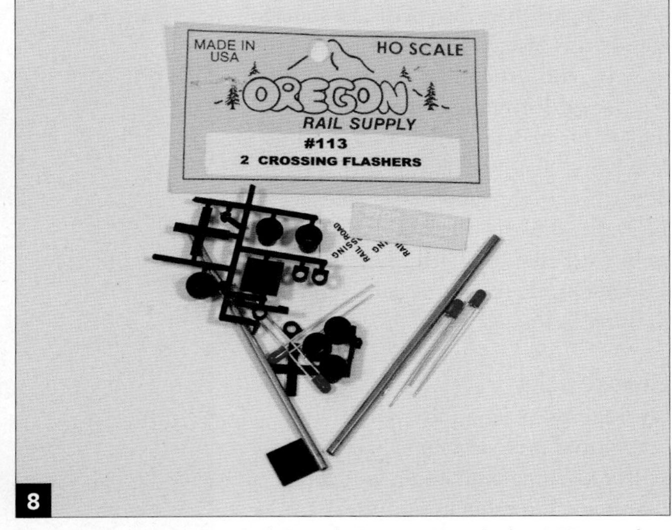

This kit from Oregon Rail Supply (no. 113) includes LEDs and enough parts to make two flashing signals.

with warm air from a hair dryer set on low heat.

Following the diagram in the kit I glued the crossarms and sign boards to the posts using cyanoacrylate adhesive (CA, or super glue), **5**. The 1954 MUTCD specified that the crossbucks be placed 10 feet above the road surface. Once the paint was dry I applied the decals including those reminding motorists of the 5 MPH speed limit in Virginia, **6**. I sealed the decals with a coat of Testor's Dullcote.

I measured back a scale 15 feet from the center line of the tracks and 6 feet from the edge of the road. Using an awl I punched holes in the foam scenery and installed the crossbucks. A couple of cars obligingly waiting at the crossbucks completed the scene and turned a barren grade crossing into a mini-vignette of a bygone era, **7**.

Flashing lights

Now let's upgrade the installation on a busier road by adding flashing lights. Although ready-to-install metal versions are available, I used a kit from Oregon Rail Supply (no. 113) which includes LEDs and parts for two complete signal lights, **8**.

Before assembly and painting, I filed openings in the brass tubes using a round file about ¾" below the top, **9**. To make painting and assembly easier I slid all the components onto the brass mast first, then glued them in place, **10**. Following the MUTCD guidelines I placed the crossbuck supports at 10 feet, and the signal lights between 7'-6" and 9'-6" above the road.

I hand-painted the crossbucks white and the banner boards and target faces black, then added decals as before. Don't install the crossbucks and banner boards until after the LEDs are installed and wired as they can be easily knocked off in the process. Using a can of Rustoleum silver wheel paint, I sprayed the assembled mast in one coat which gave it a nice metallic finish.

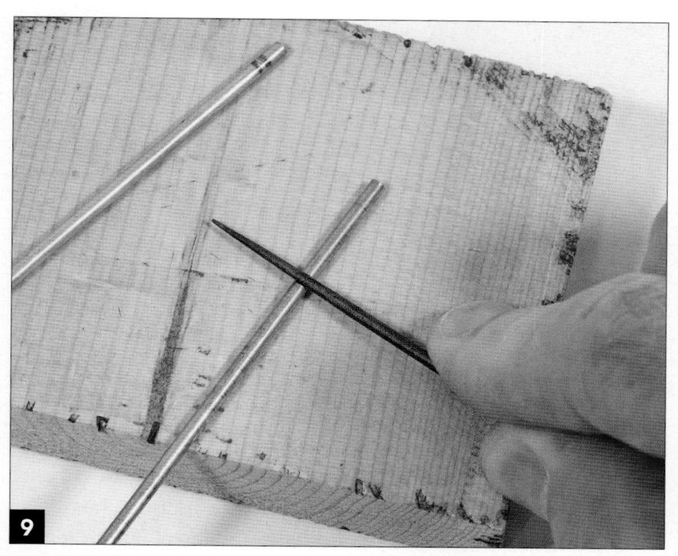

Create holes in the brass tubes using a small round file about ¾" below the top of the mast.

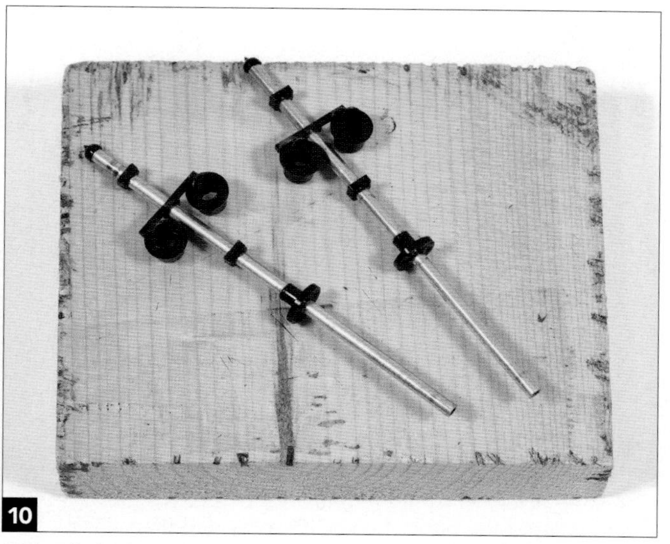

Slide all the components onto each brass mast and secure them with drops of CA.

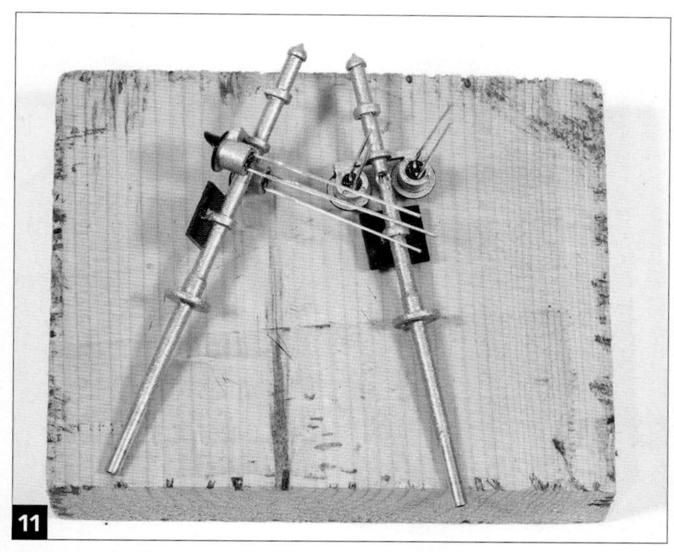

Spray-paint the assembled masts silver, then press the LEDs into the targets oriented as shown.

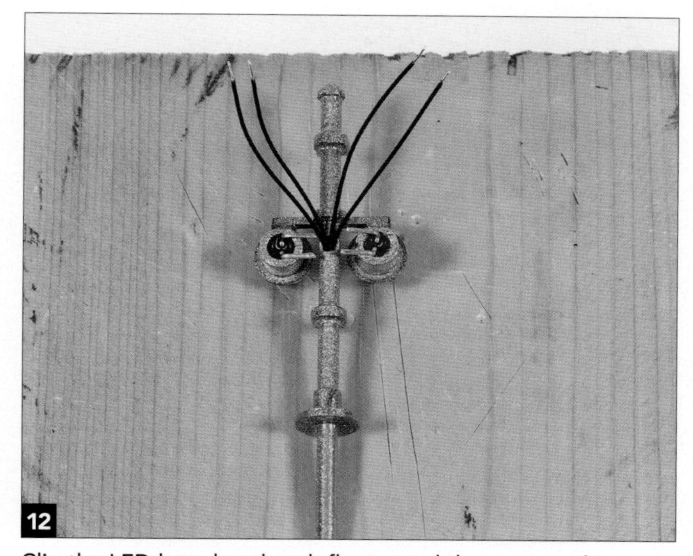

Clip the LED legs, bend each flat toward the mast, and insert the wires into the hole in the mast.

Now comes the fun part—installing the LEDs. The Oregon Rail Supply kit instructions call for common anode wiring whereas the flashing circuit I chose will not work that way. Instead you need to attach a separate wire to each lead on the LEDs. Following the instructions I inserted the LEDs into the rear of the targets, **11**, and secured them with a drop of CA. I cut each of the LED legs to about ⅛" long. I then inserted four 8" lengths of 30-gauge wire-wrap wire into the hole I had filed in the mast and slowly fed them in until they came out the bottom. This wire has a very thin insulator and it isn't difficult to work it into the mast.

I then pulled all but about 1" of each wire through the mast, **12**, soldered a wire to each, then bent it so it laid flat against the bottom of the LED. Make sure to mark the cathode (-) wires—I clipped them about ½" shorter than the anode wires. I pulled the wires from the bottom while guiding them into the mast at the top. To prevent light from leaking out and to blend them in, I hand-painted the back of each LED with gray and then silver paint, **13**.

With the paint dry I measured the locations for the signals and drilled 3⁄32" holes through the scenery and plywood base and installed the completed units, **14**. The MUTCD calls for 10-15 feet from the center line of the track and 6 feet from the roadway, but you may have to fudge a bit. In the end you have to go with what looks good and not what a technical manual specifies—just make signals clear passing locomotives and rolling stock.

Control

Several companies offer detection and control circuits for crossing flashers, including Circuitron, Rob Paisley, and the one I chose from Quickar Electronics (www.moreleds.com). Quickar actually offers two circuits, one to detect trains and a second to

13 I soldered a wire to each LED leg, and to prevent light leakage, I hand-painted the back of each LED gray and then silver.

14 After measuring the locations for the signals, I drilled holes through the scenery and plywood base and installed the masts.

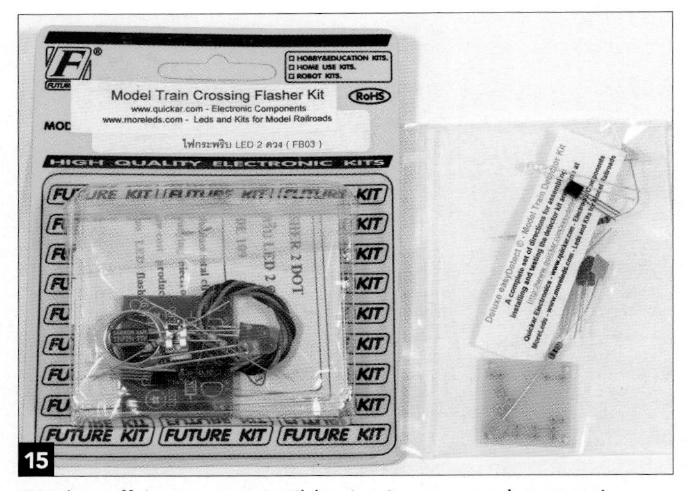

15 Quickar offers two compatible circuits: one to detect trains (left) and a second to control the flashing LEDs. Both are easy-to-assemble kits.

16 Prewiring both circuits at my workbench and mounting them to a scrap piece of lumber simplified installing them under the layout.

control the flashing LEDs, **15**. These kits are simple to build but if you are not interested in or set up for soldering, Circuitron's are ready to install.

The Quickar kits contain only a few parts each, are easy to put together, and the instructions are very detailed (you can download them from the Quickar website to get an idea). I included an entire chapter on soldering in my book *Wiring Your Model Railroad,* available from Kalmbach Books (also see the tutorial on soldering on page 92). I wired the two circuits together on my workbench, **16**, then used double-sided foam tape to attach both circuit boards and terminal strips to a small board and screwed it to the underside of the layout.

The train detectors consist of two to four phototransistors (depending on which kit version you purchase), **17**, placed between the rails on both sides of the grade crossing. When a locomotive passes over the first phototransistor, the circuit turns on the flashing LEDs and remains on until the last car clears the second phototransistor. One of the realities of using phototransistors is that the signals stay on only as long as one of the phototransistors is covered. Consequently, if a single locomotive or even a very short train passes between them the signals will stop momentarily.

One work-around is to add more phototransistors and decrease the distance between them. Since my crossing sees a lot of individual switching locomotives I added a third phototransistor, wired in series with the other two, in the middle of the crossing. You may need to experiment with your installation and operating situation. Installation requires drilling ⅛" holes between the ties at the chosen locations and inserting the prewired phototransistors up from the bottom, **18**. A small scrap of cork or styrofoam inserted in the hole will keep the phototransistor in place.

I connected the phototransistors to the detector circuit board and connected the leads from the board to the inputs on the flasher circuit board as shown in the instructions. To power the circuits I connected a positive and

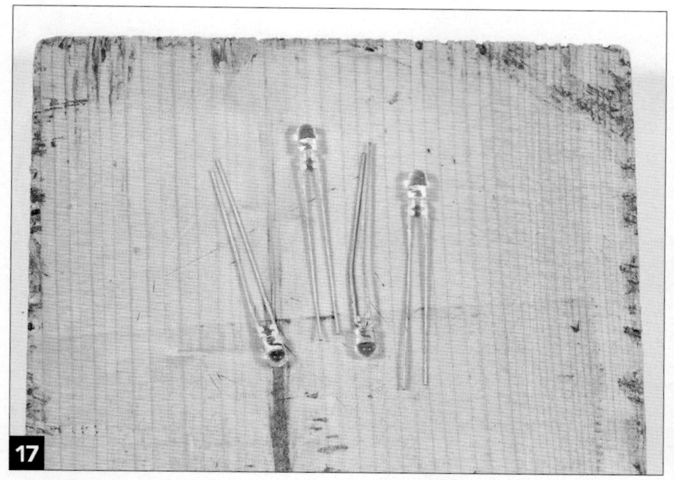

The train detector circuit is triggered by phototransistors (which look like LEDs with long leads) placed between the rails.

Drill holes between the ties at the chosen locations and insert the prewired phototransistors up from the bottom. Once installed they are almost invisible.

I installed a Woodland Scenics Just Plug pole light (see more on those in Chapter 3) to help illuminate one phototransistor. It doubles as a nice detail item as well.

One of my phototransistor detectors was under a bridge, so I installed an infrared (IR) LED directly above it, hidden under a bridge beam.

negative lead from my 12VDC power bus. It was then a simple matter to connect the wires from the signals to the circuit board. Since the Quickar circuits are designed for LEDs, separate dropping resistors aren't required. Pay close attention to the fact that the wires from the right-hand LED on each signal must be connected to the solder points on one side of the circuit, and the wires from the left LED on each signal must be connected to the other set of solder points. This arrangement creates the alternate flashing of the LEDs on each signal.

The detection circuit is designed to operate with normal layout lighting. If your flashing signals stay on continuously you may need to increase overhead illumination. The potentiometer on the detector board controls the light sensitivity while the potentiometer on the flasher board controls the flash rate of the LEDs. Turning the potentiometer on the detector clockwise increases its sensitivity. Another way to increase sensitivity is to point the phototransistor towards the closest overhead light instead of keeping it perfectly vertical. Don't overlook an opportunity to install small pole-mounted pole lights over a phototransistor to increase illumination, **19**.

If increased visible overhead lighting isn't to your liking, then you could replace the phototransistors with infrared (IR) phototransistors and use IR LEDs placed on utility poles next to the track so they are over the IR phototransistors. I found that a LPT2023 IR phototransistor from Jameco was more sensitive to my layout lights than the originals. Since humans can't see infrared light, adjusting these to get them aimed directly down on the IR phototransistor can be a problem. However, most digital camera sensors can see IR light so look at your display screen to focus the IR light pattern. Since my crossing is next to a bridge I attached an IR LED to the underside of the bridge, focused down onto the IR phototransistor there, **20**. The final installation adds a touch of realism to an otherwise static scene, **1**.

CHAPTER SIX

Crossing gates

As a train rolls through, the gates drop, lights flash, and the bells clang, warning HO motorists to stay off the tracks.

The first U. S. patent for a crossing gate was awarded in 1867 and they came into use by the late 1800s. Through the early 1900s these gates were manually operated by crossing watchmen, with automatic gates becoming common by the mid-1900s. In most cases red flashing lights and bells were also used to warn of oncoming trains, **1**.

2 The NJI kit contains a pair of crossing gates with the relay base and black-and-white striped type A gates. Red-and-white and bar gates are also available, as are N scale gates.

3 A piece of brass tubing epoxied to the relay base provides a firm mounting support.

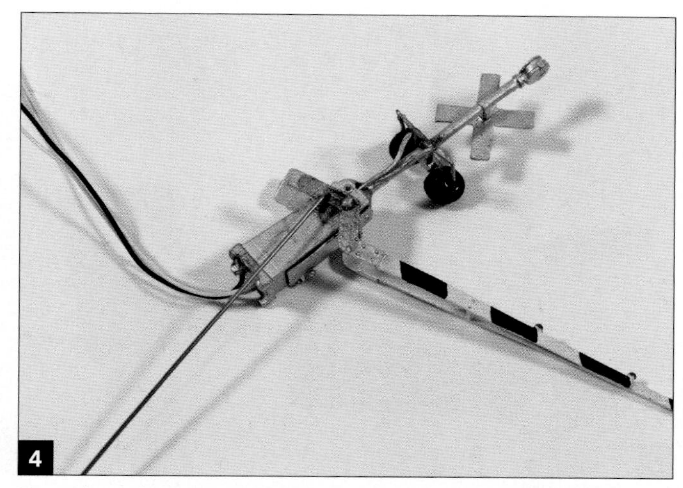

4 To replace the original actuator rod, I drilled a .028" hole in the gate arm right behind the pivot point and installed a piece of .025" wire.

Crossing gates were located like crossbucks as described in Chapter 1, and the *Manual on Uniform Traffic Control Devices* (MUTCD) specified the height of the closed gate above the pavement at 3 feet. Gates typically had black and white stripes into the early 1970s, but in 1971 the MUTCD mandated a change to red and white stripes. It's a good idea to check photos of crossings in the area and era you model.

For my HO crossing I chose an NJ International model (they make flashers and gates in N scale as well). This gate is offered with either a relay case or pedestal base and a type A or bar type gate. The type A gate is constructed of two pieces of wood whereas the bar type is a single piece of wood. I selected the no. 1161, which contains a pair of crossing gates with the relay base, type A gate, and black and white stripes, **2**.

Mechanisms

The relay base offers no means of mounting the unit—it just sits flat on the layout with the wires and actuating rod dangling down. To remedy this I cut a 1½" piece of ⅜" diameter brass tubing and epoxied it into the relay base after feeding the wires through it, **3**. I then measured the proper scale distances from the tracks and road and drilled a ⅜"-diameter mounting hole. With the brass tube inserted in the hole it provided a stable installation. However, it also pointed out another problem.

With the first gate in place I got under the layout and started making measurements for the Circuitron remote activator. However, the actuating rod on the crossing gate wasn't long enough to reach—apparently my 1"-thick foam and plywood sandwich was more than the manufacturer planned for. My first reaction was to attempt to replace the actuating wire with a longer one, but in the process I broke off the connecting pin inside the unit.

As a replacement I drilled a .028" hole in the gate arm right behind the pivot point and installed a piece of .025" wire to serve as the actuating rod, **4**. This can be on either side of the relay base to keep it out of sight. If you have to do this, it is important to keep

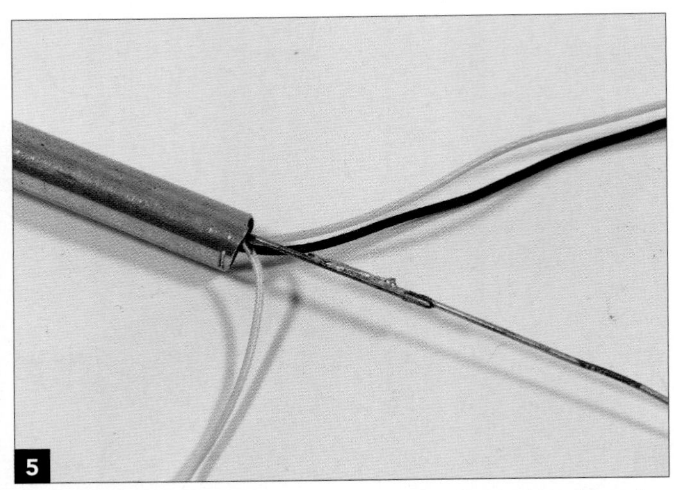
On the second signal, to extend the actuating rod I soldered to it a piece of .020" brass wire.

The Circuitron remote activator and bell crank kit allow controlling two separate crossing gates with one Tortoise.

The completed remote signal activator (left) and bellcrank (right) are smooth-operating mechanisms.

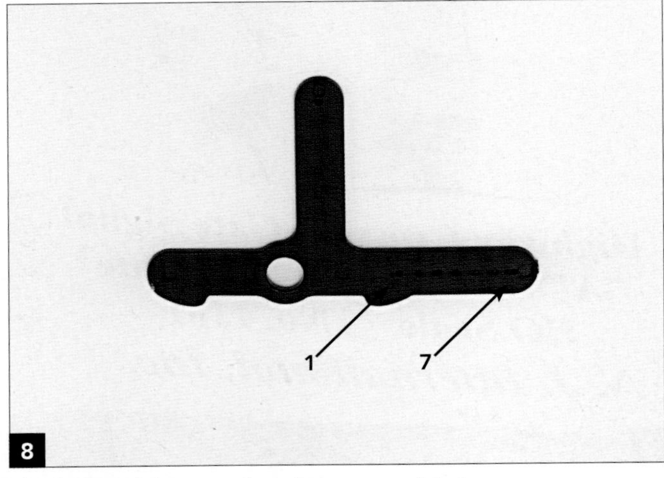

The bellcrank has a series of seven small holes on one arm numbered in increasing order from the large pivot hole near the center.

the wire attachment point as close to the pivot point as possible so the throw distance of the actuating rod will be essentially the same for both crossing gates.

Since the actuating rod is .020" brass wire, on the second gate I sanded the ends of the actuating rod and a second piece of .020" brass wire and clamped them next to one another with a hemostat. I applied flux and soldered them together, creating a solid joint, **5**. Finally I was able to install both crossing gates and proceed to installing the Circuitron remote signal activator and Tortoise switch machine.

The Circuitron remote activator (800-8100) along with an additional bell crank kit (800-8101) allows you to control up to two separate crossing gates, **6**. The instructions, although lengthy and seemingly complex, are presented in a logical step-by-step manner which makes the installation easier than it appears. I didn't find any steps confusing: Just go slow, don't jump ahead or try to do it another way and the end result should be perfect, **7**. The critical steps are getting the correct measurement of the length of throw for the gate mechanism and making the adjustment for the end of throw on the remote actuator.

To measure the length of throw I had a helper hold the gate in the full upright position while I made a mark on the rod with a fine-point marker at the point where it exited the brass tube. I then had my helper hold the gate in its lowered horizontal position while I measured the distance between the bottom of the brass tube and the mark I had made on the actuator rod. This was .118", which was a bit less than the .135" value for this crossing gate given in the instructions. However this difference is due to the fact I was not measuring the total throw distance. At any rate I finally settled on using the larger value. Next you need to look at the table provided in the instructions and select a drive mechanism pivot hole number and a corresponding bellcrank hole number. In this case these were 3 and 2, respectively.

The bellcrank is a T-shaped piece with a series of 7 small holes on one arm, **8**. The wire actuator on the crossing gate will be inserted into one of these 7 holes—the specific

Automatic crossing gates, together with flashing lights, protect most busy crossings on modern main lines.

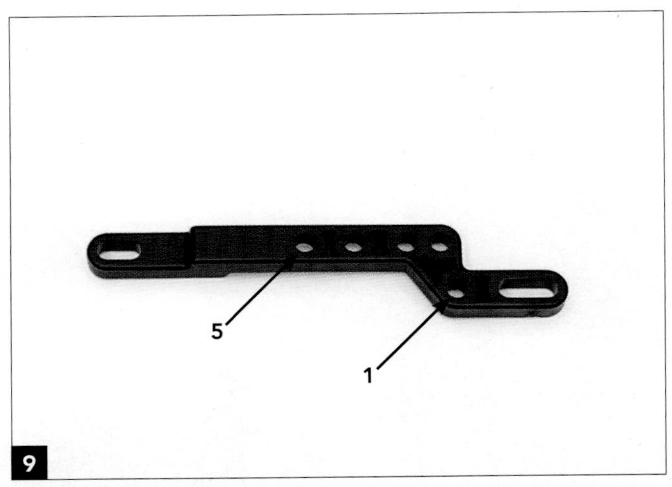

9

The drive mechanism pivot holes are numbered in increasing order from the slide end of the drive arm (right).

10

The screws on the bellcrank mounting plate make final adjustments an easy process.

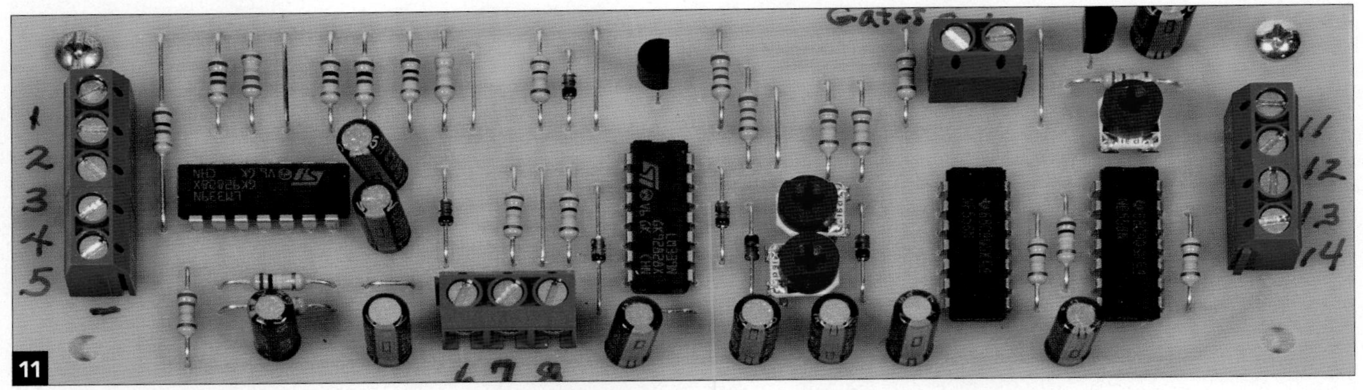

11

The boards are offered in kit form as well as assembled (above).

hole was determined from the chart just mentioned. I decided to use hole number 2, the second hole out from the large pivot hole on the center. The drive mechanism pivot holes are numbered in increasing order from the slide end of the drive arm, **9**. Notice that the arm has an "L" in it: Holes 1 and 2 are on the base of the L and holes 3-5 are on the long portion of the arm. It's critical to get the order of these holes correct in order for the mechanism to function as designed.

With the remote signal activator and both bellcrank assemblies completed and installed under the layout, I used a 12VDC power supply to test the action of the crossing gates and make final adjustments following the instructions. The pair of adjustment screws on the bellcrank mounting plate, **10**, make this easy. By moving these screws in or out you can set the stopping point for the bellcrank arm on each throw of the Tortoise and control exactly stopped position of the crossing gates. The instructions also include useful tips on how to adjust the activator slides so that the midpoint of each crossing gate is synchronized with the midpoint of the Tortoise throw.

Control circuits

Many companies offer kits, assembled circuit boards, and train detectors to control crossing gates. I chose a circuit board from Rob Paisley. His website (home.cogeco.ca/~rpaisley4/CircuitIndex.html) provides a myriad of electronic circuits for model railroaders. His crossing gate control circuit is available as either a bare board, a kit with all the components, or as an assembled and tested unit. It uses infrared phototransistors (which also respond to visible light) as between-the-rails detectors to trigger the gate closing and opening.

In addition to driving the Tortoise switch machine used in the Circuitron remote activator, it also has a flashing circuit for the LEDs. There's also an optional add-on circuit board that will operate a bell. Since the assembled boards were only a dollar more than the kit I chose that option, **11**.

I drilled ⅛" holes at the locations shown in Rob's instructions and installed the phototransistors. This step is essentially the same as for the flashing crossbucks in Chapter 5 except more phototransistors are involved. Pay close attention to the information on Rob's website for tips on locating the phototransistors.

Like the phototransistor detectors in Chapter 5, these may also be sensitive to extreme low-light conditions, although Rob did say that they perform well under most layout lighting. If you have problems, you can add infrared LEDs directly over the phototransistors.

The bell I used is an old-fashioned doorbell with a clapper. I bought it on

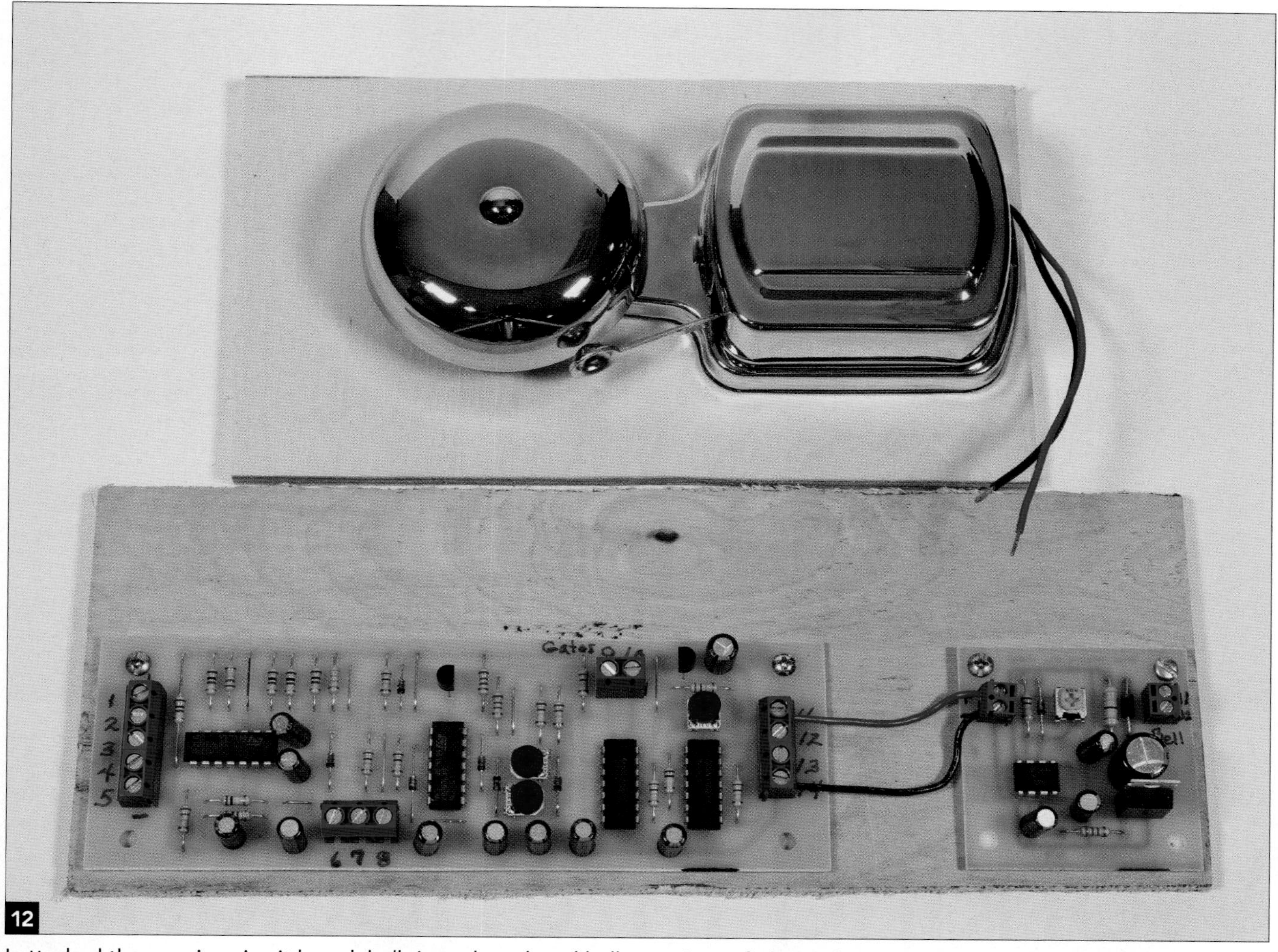

12

I attached the crossing circuit board, bell ringer board, and bell to a piece of plywood, pre-wired as much as possible on the workbench, then screwed it under the layout.

eBay (a Thomas and Betts Carlon 2½" chrome doorbell). The bell can get very annoying if it remains on very long, so I added an SPST toggle switch on the fascia to turn it off. This is simply wired into one of the wires going to the bell. Slight tuning adjustments can be made to the bell by bending the clapper arm.

Finally, I attached the circuit boards and bell to a piece of plywood and pre-wired as much as possible on the workbench, **12**, then screwed it to the underside of the layout. Following the wiring diagram I connected the phototransistors, flashing LEDs, and Tortoise to the main circuit board and connected the 12VDC power from my supply bus.

Be sure to pay close attention to the type of wiring used with your crossing gates as some use common anode and others common cathode. The instructions specify wiring each type. With the power and circuit turned on, I ran a train through the crossing and it sprang to life with flashing lights, clanging bell, and gates dropping, **1**.

Control on multiple tracks

One thing to consider when selecting a crossing gate controller is whether it will detect trains on only one track or two. With Rob's design you can use a second circuit board to have independent control on either track, or simply daisy-chain the detectors with only one board. Because the detectors overlap this way, two trains cannot pass through the protected section and activate the gates properly unless one of them is in the crossing and covering one of the stop sensors. However, as long as trains only pass through the detectors one at a time, in both directions, or if one train is already in the grade crossing, then the circuit will act properly. Only you can decide whether your traffic pattern will require a second circuit board. There is extensive information on Rob's website to help you decide. You can also install a single board and add a second one later if you are not satisfied with the single board approach.

CHAPTER SEVEN

Working interlocking semaphore signal

With a Southern passenger train rolling across the diamonds, the home interlocking signal on the C&O main line is at horizontal, meaning "stop."

Semaphore signals began appearing in the U. S. about 1860. Color-light signals came into use by the mid-1900s, and by the late 1900s semaphores had become rare, but many that remained were at interlockings, **1**, junctions where tracks cross and routes diverge.

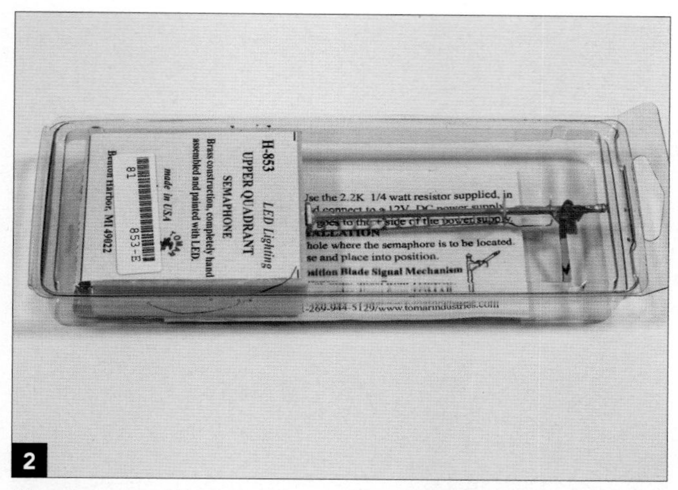

2 Many brass ready-to-install semaphores are available in several scales, including this Tomar HO scale single-arm signal. Tomar models have moving blades controlled by actuating wires.

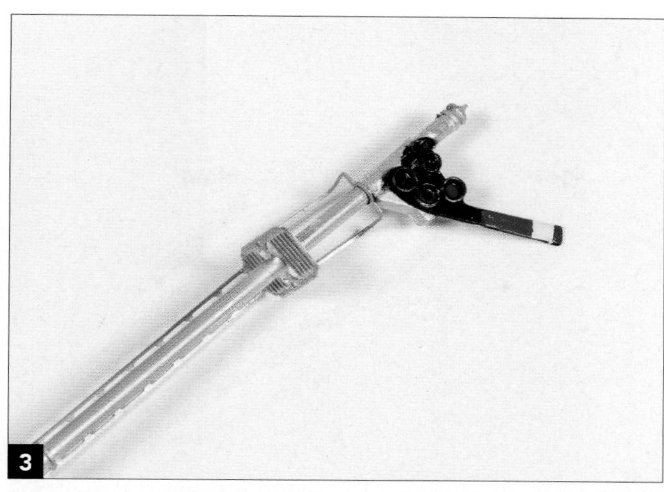

3 To modify the end of the blade, I trimmed it using Xuron track cutters, sanded the end smooth, and repainted it to match the prototype.

4 To provide the semaphore mast a stable base I cut out a 1" square in the foam scenery base and glued a square of ½" wood in its place.

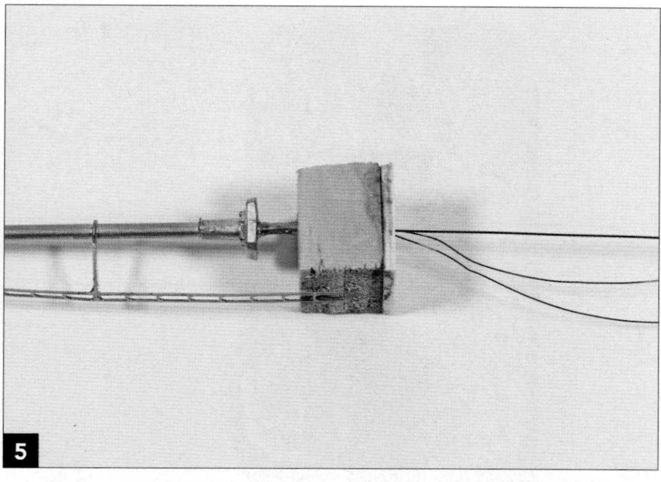

5 I drilled a hole through the wood to match the post diameter and gave the semaphore a test fit. The lenses are illuminated by an LED; the leads and actuating wire are at right.

Semaphores typically consist of a movable arm or blade that can be positioned at three indications or angles: horizontal, 45 degrees, and vertical. If the blades move upward from horizontal they are referred to as upper-quadrant semaphores; if they move downward they are lower-quadrant (lower-quadrant signals typically have just two indications). Semaphores have three colored glass lenses at their base: red, yellow, and green, all illuminated by a single bulb. As the blade moves, the correct color lens aligns with the light bulb. Horizontal (red) means stop; 45 degrees (yellow) is restricted or caution; vertical (green) means clear.

Modeling a semaphore installation can range from installing inexpensive nonfunctional plastic models to fully operational brass models with working lights and independently controlled arms, **2**. The cost of a fully functional semaphore installation operated by a slow-motion motor can get expensive, but they add a lot of realism to a depot or interlocking tower scene.

One inexpensive mechanism for operating a semaphore is a pushrod assembly like those used with Blue Point switch machines or Hump Yard Purveyance levers (www.humpyard.com). A motorized option is the Circuitron kit that uses a Tortoise switch machine to move the arms. This is available with only two stops for the green and red positions, which I used for this project. A second version controlled by an electronic circuit board provides fully indexed stops for all three positions.

On my HO scale Piedmont Southern I have a major crossing at Charlottesville, Va., where the Chesapeake & Ohio single-track main crosses the Southern's double-track line. Until about 1965 this crossing was protected by a manned interlocking tower with semaphores on each side of the tower. To model this crossing I decided to install a single-arm semaphore on the C&O side and a double-arm semaphore on the Southern side. The two arms are necessary to signal trains approaching the crossing from opposite directions on opposite

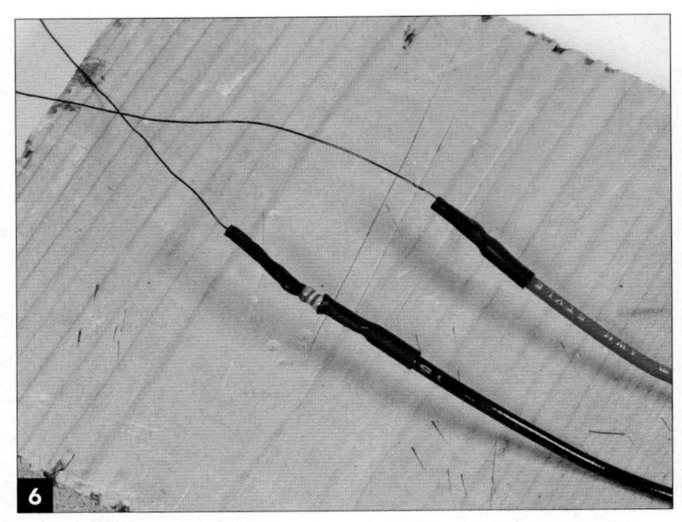

I soldered 6"-long red and black wires to the wires extending from the semaphore base, with a resistor on the black wire.

Some dirt, gravel, and ground foam completed the visible portions of the installation.

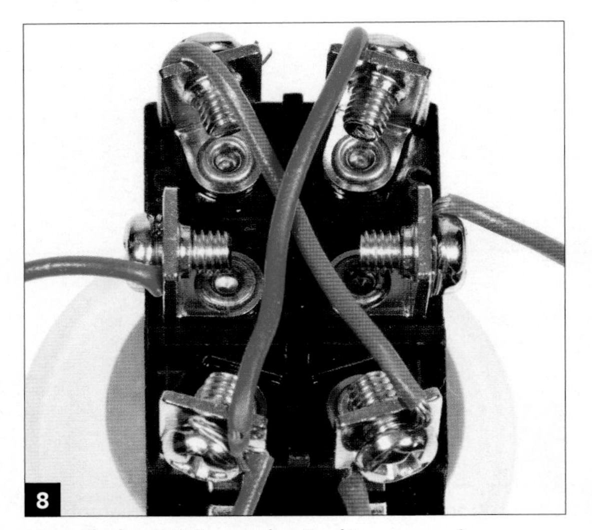

I installed a DPDT switch wired in a reversing pattern in the fascia near the semaphore.

A T-tap connector makes it a quick and easy job to connect accessories.

tracks. (The Southern at this time followed a right-hand running rule on its double-track main line). Let's take a look at the C&O signal installation.

Basic installation

I used an assembled upper-quadrant semaphore from Tomar (no. H-853), **2**. The model comes painted with a pre-wired LED and an actuating rod, making this an easy installation. The arm had the wrong colors for my prototype and had a pointed end—the prototype C&O arm was red and white with a square end. This was an easy fix. I trimmed the end with Xuron track cutters, sanded the end smooth, and repainted it to match the prototype, **3**.

The brass mounting rod that extends below the base of the semaphore was too short to go through both my ½"-thick foam scenery base and the ½" plywood underneath. To give the semaphore a stable base I cut out a 1" square in the foam scenery base and glued a square of ½" wood in its place, **4**. I drilled a ⅛" diameter hole through the wood insert and gave the semaphore a test fit, **5**.

Before proceeding further I soldered the 680-ohm resistor provided with the semaphore to the black wire and temporarily connected a 12VDC power supply to the resistor and red wire. Always make sure everything works before installing components! After confirming the LED worked, I soldered 6"-long red and black wires to the red and black wires extending from the semaphore base, **6**. This makes it easier to make the final connections under the layout. Protect the soldered connections with heat-shrink tubing. Finally, I fed the wires and pushrod through the hole, inserted the brass rod, and glued the semaphore base in place. Some dirt and ground foam completed the visible portions of the installation, **7**.

Wiring and motion

I wired a double-pole, double-throw (DPDT) toggle switch in a reversing pattern, **8**, and mounted it on the fascia near the semaphore. (You can use either a toggle or a slide switch as long as it is DPDT.) First solder or screw

A double-arm semaphore indicates "stop" for the Southern Pacific branch line where it crosses the Missouri-Kansas-Texas at San Antonio, Texas, in 1954. *Philip R. Hastings*

Circuitron's remote signal activator uses a Tortoise switch machine to move the arms.

The Tortoise moved the semaphore arm to to vertical position and displayed a green light. A quick flip of the toggle switch reversed the Tortoise and moved the arm to the horizontal position with the red light showing.

crossing wires between the two poles at each end of the switch (the ones forming an X). Next connect the two wires that will run to the power source to the two poles at one end of the switch. Finally connect the two wires that will feed electricity to the Tortoise motor to the two center poles.

When the toggle is thrown to engage the poles at the end where power is fed in, the wires that feed out from the center poles get the same polarity as that coming in to the switch. When the toggle is thrown in the opposite direction, the polarity to the center poles is reversed due to the crossing wires. This simple circuit has many uses, and has been used by model railroaders for decades.

With the DPDT switch installed, I made the connection to the 12VDC power supply bus under the layout (I have a power bus strictly just for powering accessories). A T-tap connector makes it a quick and easy job of connecting wires while allowing them to be disconnected later for trouble-shooting, replacement, or maintenance, **9**. I turned on the power to make sure the LED was still working, then moved to the control mechanism.

For this installation I only needed two (red and green) arm positions, so I opted for the Circuitron 800-8100 actuator kit. This mechanism is powered by a Tortoise switch machine and has positive stops at each end of the throw, providing the two arm positions. I assembled the kit just as described in Chapter 6 and installed it under the semaphore, **10**. The Tortoise can then be wired to the DPDT switch installed in the fascia and installed in the bracket. When the power was turned on the Tortoise moved the semaphore arm to to vertical position and displayed a green light, **11**. A quick flip of the toggle reversed the Tortoise and moved the arm to the horizontal position with the red light showing, **1**.

You can wire a full interlocking junction with separate controls for each signal, or wire the signals together so that flipping one toggle switch clears one route while setting the signals on the other route to "stop."

1

CHAPTER EIGHT

Installing and wiring a turntable

A turntable can be the centerpiece of a locomotive servicing terminal. Turntables (and their attached tracks and roundhouses) can take up a lot of space, but they provide fascinating animation and they're great for showing off locomotives, **1**.

Turntables were the popular option to get steam locomotives headed in the right direction. Even though they take up a lot of room on a model railroad, they are eye-catching and can be featured attractions of many locomotive servicing scenes. This is a scene in progress on my HO Piedmont Southern.

I used a 105-foot-diameter turntable and pit that I bought in kit form from Custom Model Railroads.

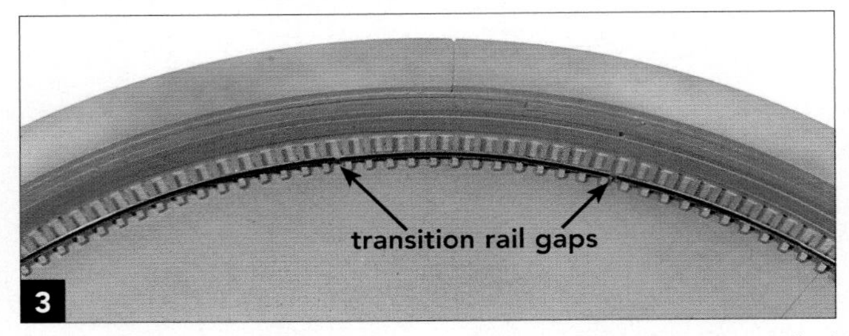

The only tricky part of installation is getting the pit rail installed with its pair of transition rails—keep the rail gaps small.

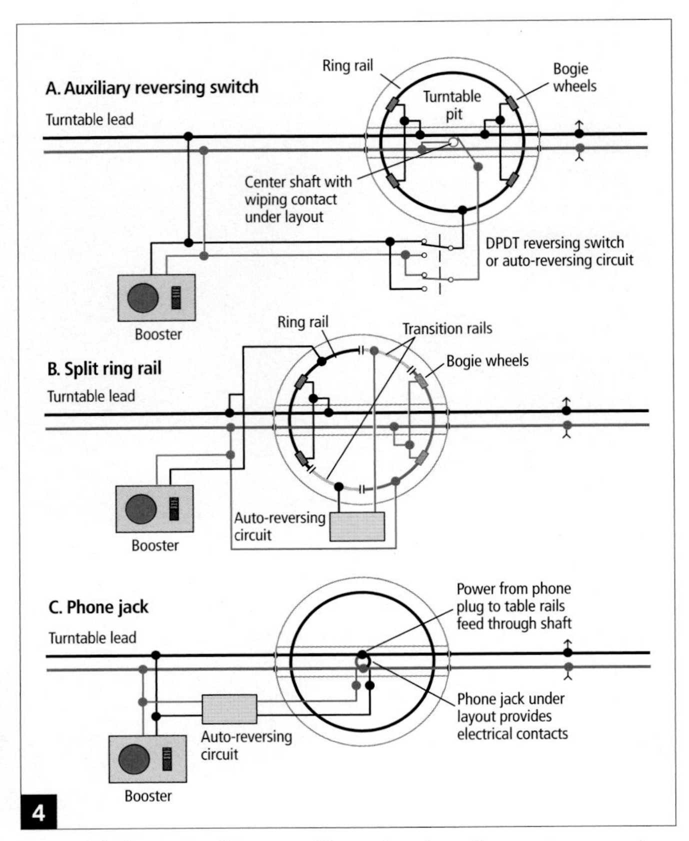

To avoid short circuits you will need to install an auto-reversing circuit using one of these methods. I chose option B. These methods may not be needed with DCC-compatible models

Begin installation by marking the point on the plywood of the exact center of the turntable.

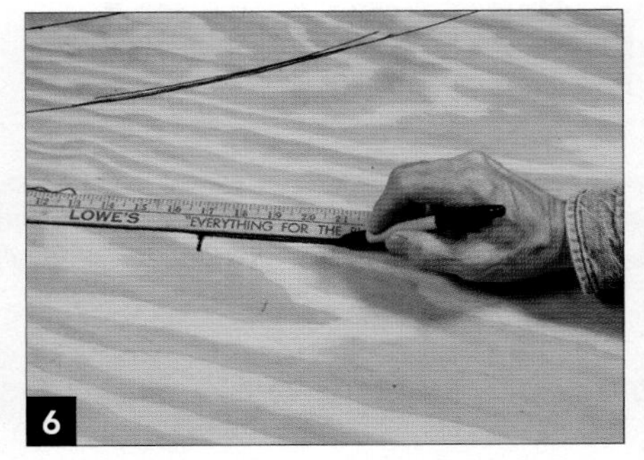

Lay out the centerline of the approach track and and any other tracks that will be meeting the turntable, extending the lines through the turntable center.

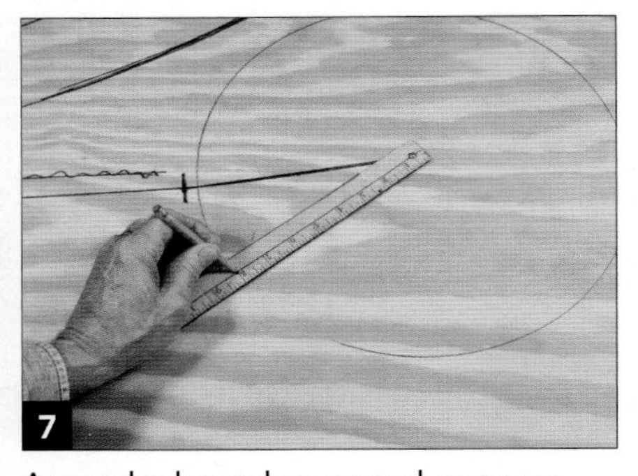

A wood ruler makes a good compass. Insert a wood screw in one hole and the tip of a sharp pencil in the second hole and mark the turntable circle.

There are a number of prebuilt and kit turntables available in a range of sizes including Digital Command Control (DCC) compatible models from Walthers and others. If you are into scratchbuilding, there have been a number of construction articles over the years in *Model Railroader* and other hobby magazines.

I have a 105-foot turntable and pit, **2**, that I built from a kit made by Custom Model Railroads (CMR, www.custommodelrailroads.com). For this project I'll show you how I installed it on the Piedmont Southern. These kits are available in 90-, 105-, 120-, and 135-foot diameters. The techniques I show will be similar to what is required for other models as well.

The CMR kit is made of laser-cut acrylic sheet and very easy to assemble: just pop out all the parts and stack them as described in the instructions, gluing them together as you go. The only tricky part is getting the pit rail installed. The transition rail gaps, **3**, are touchy since the turntable bogie wheels are small in diameter and will catch in the gaps if the gaps are too large. You're better off making the gaps too small and enlarging them if needed.

The transition rails also are an important part of wiring the turntable to prevent short circuits with DCC. To avoid short circuits as the turntable rotates you will need to install an auto-

8

Double-check the diameter of the circle, then carefully cut along the line with a saber saw (make sure the area underneath is clear). Test-fit the turntable pit.

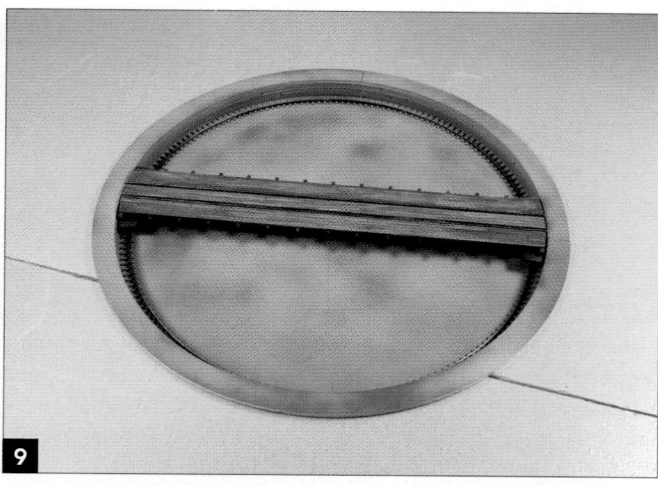

9

After marking the location for the pit opening on the ½" foam sheet, I cut it out, glued the sheet in place on the plywood using Liquid Nails for Projects, and test-fit the turntable.

reversing circuit such as those shown in **4**. These circuits will detect when the electrical pickups on the turntable cross from the long pit rails to the short transition sections and correct the polarity instantly. I discussed the details of this topic in my book *Wiring Your Model Railroad* and also in the February 2018 *Model Railroader*.

I'm assuming you will have done all your planning for the arrangement of your roundhouse, coaling tower, ashpit, and other associated structures and know exactly where you want the turntable located. Because this section on my layout has to lift out for access to my breaker panel, I was able to do most of the cutting and fitting on sawhorses.

Restored Norfolk & Western J-class 4-8-4 no. 611 goes for a spin on the turntable at Spencer, N.C. The big locomotive barely fits on the table. *Jim Wrinn*

First, after placing the pit assembly where I wanted the finished turntable, I marked the exact centerpoint on the plywood, **5**. I then laid out the centerline of the approach track and extended it through where the turntable was to be installed, **6**. Next I measured the diameter of the underside of the turntable pit—this told me how big a hole in the layout would be necessary into which to drop the pit. If there are any supporting joists directly under the turntable location they may need to be relocated prior to cutting the hole.

Given the diameter of the pit, I made a trammel with an old yardstick, but an old scrap of stripwood will do. This should be a little longer than one-half the diameter of the pit. I then drilled a hole at one end of the stick just big enough for a small screw to pass through. After marking the position for another hole at the other end of the stick at one-half the pit diameter, I drilled a hole big enough for a pencil tip to fit in. Placing the trammel on the plywood with the first hole over the center point of the pit, I inserted a small wood screw. I inserted the tip of a sharp pencil in the second hole and marked a 360 degree circle on the plywood, **7**.

I drilled a ⅜" diameter hole just inside the circle and used it as a starter hole for a jigsaw. Cutting along the line I removed the outlined circle, **8**. I placed a piece of ½" foam insulation in place on the plywood and marked the cutout from below using a marker. I then flipped the sheet over and cut out the foam inside the line. Finally I spread Liquid Nails for Projects construction adhesive on the plywood and set the foam sheet on top, **9**.

The CMR turntable pit has a lip along the top which hides the edge of the opening. However it will not support the full weight of the turntable plus a locomotive, so it needs to be supported by a base below the pit floor. For this I used the plywood circle I had just cut out. For starters I drilled a ½" hole in the center for the motor

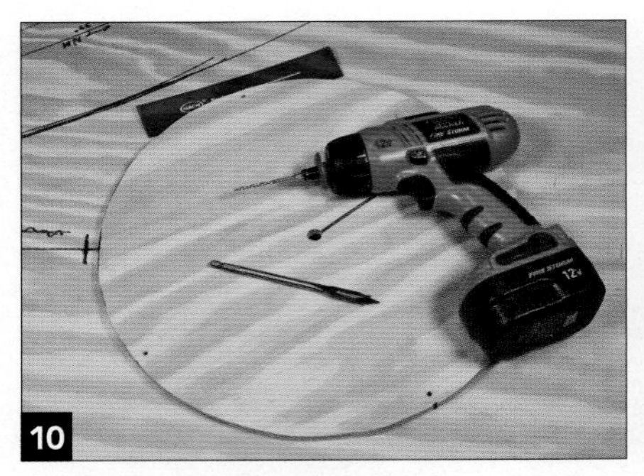

I drilled holes for the feeder wires around the perimeter of the base and a ½" diameter hole in the center for the motor shaft.

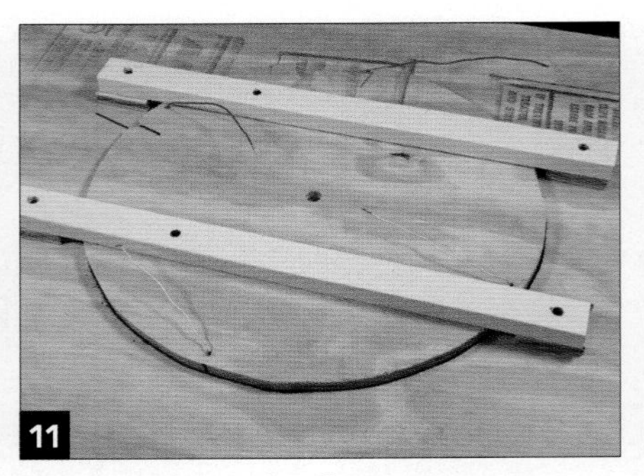

I installed a couple of support joists on spacers to suspend the base 1.5" below the layout (foam) surface. The distance depends on pit dimensions.

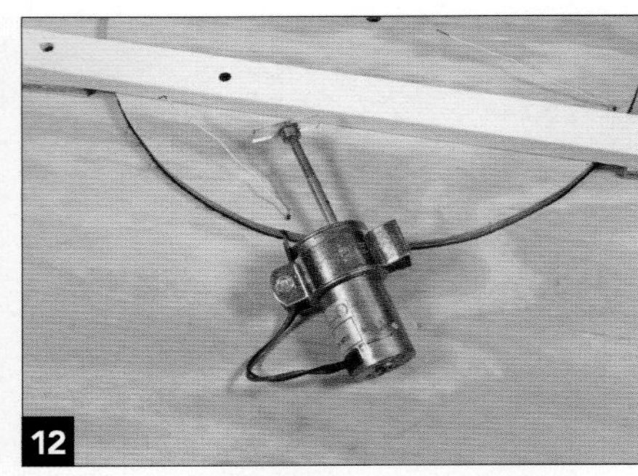

A slow-motion DC reduction-gear motor connected directly to the shaft on the turntable provides power.

A conduit hanger clamp is installed on the body of the motor and attached to a small steel L bracket. The bracket, in turn, is screwed to a wood block. This keeps the motor perpendicular to the turntable.

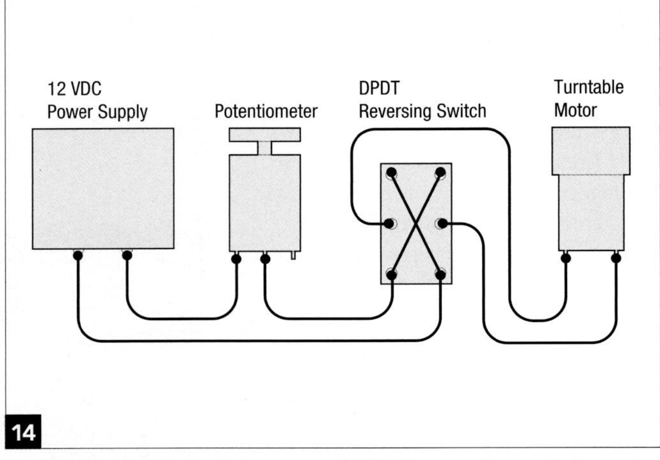

I connected a potentiometer and DPDT reversing switch between the 12VDC power supply and turntable motor. The pot controls the speed and the reversing switch allows changing the direction of rotation.

shaft bushing, and ⅛" holes for the pit rail feeders, **10**. Next I supported it with two joists to suspend it about 1.5" below the layout surface, **11**, then dropped the turntable into position.

With the turntable pit ready it was time to provide for power and motorize the turntable. I powered mine with a surplus slow-motion DC reduction gear motor connected directly to the shaft on the turntable, **12**. Jameco (www.jameco.com) has a wide selection of similar motors. Power is from a 12VDC supply bus using a potentiometer for speed control. I chose a 10K-ohm linear potentiometer with a built in on/off switch. Other options would be to use an old DC power pack or a DCC mobile decoder. On the more expensive side are the motor kits that CMR offers or the fully indexing unit from New York Railway Supply (www.nyrs.com). In my case since I only use the turntable for reversing locomotives I didn't need the indexing option.

I slipped a brass sleeve over the motor drive shaft and the brass tube attached to the turntable and secured it using set screws installed in the brass tube. Another option is to place a piece of vinyl tubing, available at most hardware stores, on the turntable shaft connecting it to the motor shaft. This is easier and less likely to work loose than the set screws. After installing a conduit hanger clamp on the body of the motor, I attached it to a steel L bracket and wood block and then screwed it to the plywood base using wood screws, **13**. To reduce transmission of motor sound to the benchwork you might want to insert a rubber pad under the mounting block or around the motor—I cut mine from an old inner tube.

With the motor installed I connected the 12VDC wires to the potentiometer, then connected it to a double-pole, double-throw (DPDT) reversing switch, both mounted in the fascia, **14**. The switch reverses the direction of rotation. Using a center-off switch will give you another way to cut power to the turntable motor. Either slide or toggle switches will work.

Finally I connected the wires from the pit rail to the track power bus and the autoreversing circuit, then placed a locomotive onto the turntable. I eased the potentiometer to the on position and increased power as the locomotive began to rotate. Now my Norfolk & Western J-class locomotives have a way to turn around for their trip back to Roanoke.

CHAPTER NINE

Electromagnetic uncouplers

Many model railroaders use under-track or between-rails magnets to uncouple cars and locomotives. They're inexpensive and easy to install, but a problem with these permanent magnets is that if a train stops above one—or is even moving very slowly—couplers may separate unexpectedly. This may not be a big issue in a yard or on a siding, but it's quite annoying on a main line.

Kadee electromagnetic uncouplers eliminate unwanted uncoupling with magnetic knuckle uncouplers and can be hidden under ballast. A white marker post helps train crews locate magnets.

Kadee electromagnetic uncouplers come in kit form, but are easy to assemble.

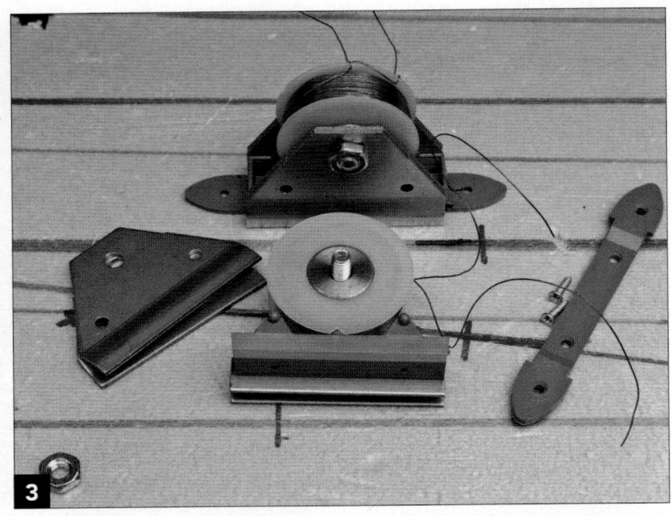
Run the long bolt through the various components (bottom assembly) and secure with the nut (top, assembled).

Attach the mounting plate with the two small wood screws.

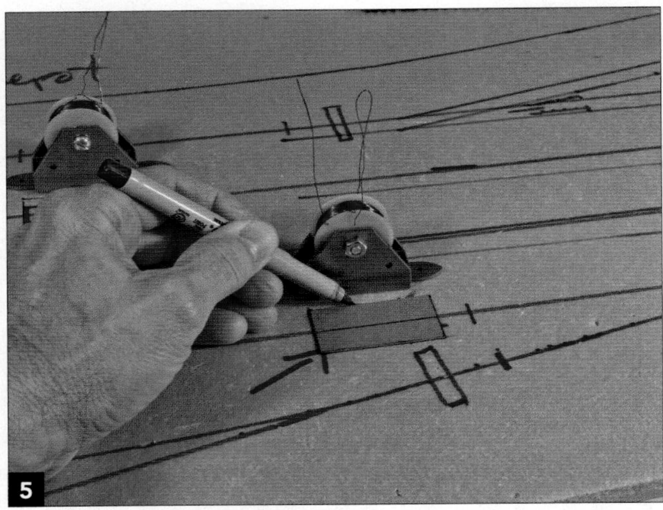
I made a cardboard template to mark the locations for the electromagnets.

One option developed by Kadee is an electromagnet. These are energized only when you want them to be, and are strong enough to be hidden under the ties, **1**. Using electromagnetic uncouplers on main lines helps eliminate unexpected train separations. They can be placed near industrial spurs, at locations where head-end cars are cut out of passenger trains, or where locomotives need to be swapped out or serviced.

Kadee electromagnetic uncouplers come in a kit form, **2**, but are simple to put together. Following the instructions, first install the round metal core into the opening in the electromagnet. Next assemble the steel field plates so that the flared upper sections face away from each other. Then insert the bolt into one set of field plates, through the electromagnet coil, and then through the other pair of field plates. Insert the plastic field plate divider between them, then secure with a nut, **3**. Note that the small notch in the electromagnet's plastic spool aligns with the small prong on the field plate divider. Attach the mounting plate with the two small wood screws. You can see the top and bottom in **4**.

Although it's possible to cut out a section of track and roadbed to install these uncouplers after track has been laid, it's a lot easier if done as part of layout construction. When installing them I lay out the track plan in the area I am working on and then place locomotives and cars on the track lines. This allows me to decide the ideal locations while avoiding turnouts and support girders under the layout.

Installation

I use ½" thick foam board over ½" plywood for my HO layout, and I draw the entire track plan and other details on the foam surface with markers. I made a 1¹⁄₁₆" x 2⅛" cardboard template to mark the locations for the electromagnets, **5**. I use a sharp knife to cut out the opening in the foam, then drill through the plywood using a ⅜" drill bit. By drilling holes in each corner of the opening I can insert a jigsaw blade and complete the hole, **6**.

Install the roadbed. I use cork

Drill ¼" holes in each corner of the opening, then insert a jigsaw blade and cut the hole in the plywood.

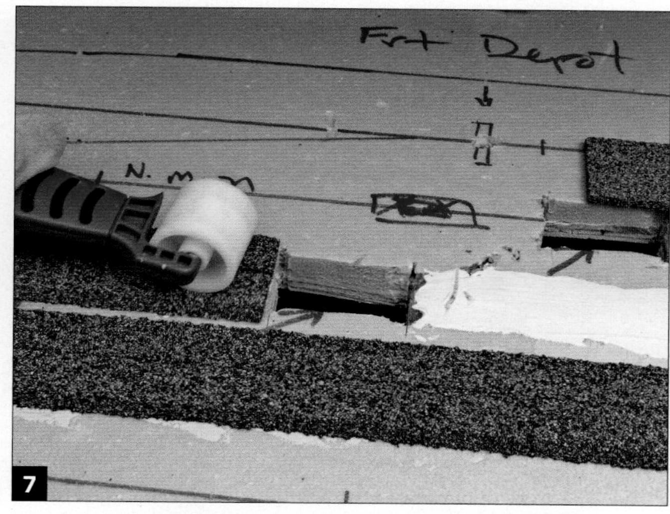

I ran a bead of adhesive along the centerline of the track, smoothed it with a putty knife, then rolled the cork in place.

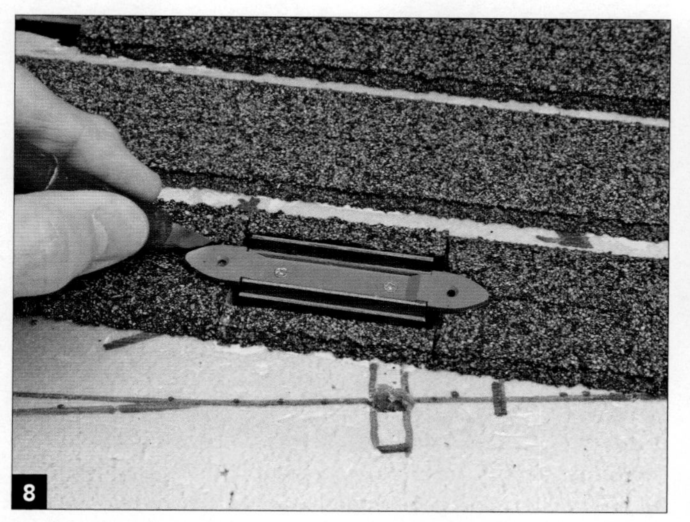

Outline the electromagnet with a marking pen, then use a knife to cut along the lines in the cork.

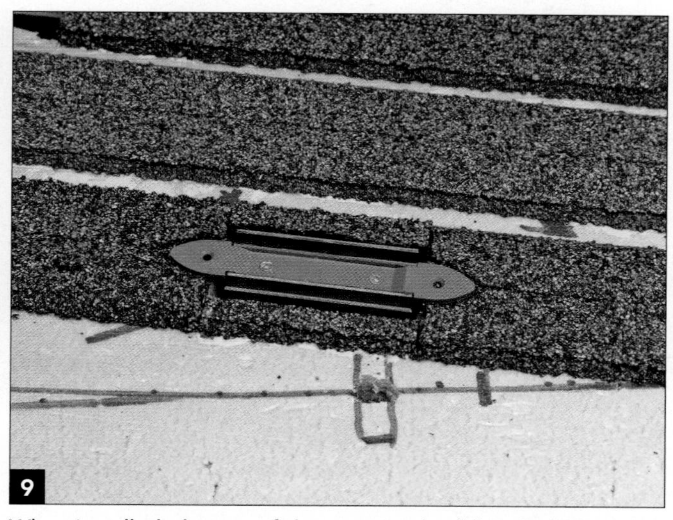

When installed, the top of the magnet should sit flush with the top of the cork.

roadbed that I glue in place using Liquid Nails for Projects construction adhesive, which is compatible with the foam. I run a bead along the centerline of the track, smooth it with a putty knife, and then lay the cork roadbed in place, leaving the openings for the electromagnets uncovered. I finish off by rolling over it with a wallpaper seam sealer, **7**, and let it dry 24 hours. I then cut pieces of the sloped edges from scraps of roadbed and glue them in place alongside the cutout.

Once the roadbed is in place I drop the electromagnets into the openings and use a marker to outline the tapered ends of the plastic supports, **8**, then I cut out the cork with a knife. Removing this cork leaves a perfect recess for the electromagnet, which will sit flush with the top of the roadbed, **9**.

Once the electromagnet is installed, power it up and test it before ballasting. Once I confirm that everything is working properly, I glue a piece of aluminum foil over the electromagnet and out onto the roadbed, **10**. This protects the magnet from glue and ballast but will not interfere with the electromagnetic field.

To lay track I again use Liquid Nails for Projects, laying a bead on the centerline of the cork and smoothing it with a putty knife. I lay the flextrack, carefully placing it atop the glue, straighten it with a yardstick, then roll it, **11**. I then ballast the track as I normally would.

Wiring

Kadee's instructions provide excellent wiring diagrams. Kadee recommends a 16V, 3A DC or 18V, 2A AC power supply to operate these—an old power pack usually isn't powerful enough. During operation, be careful not to apply power for more than about 30 seconds—any longer and you run the risk of burning through the insulation on the wires, creating a short circuit.

A simple momentary contact pushbutton switch will keep the electromagnet powered as long as it is pushed—but how can you help let your crew members know how long they've held the button down? It can also get awkward when you're holding the button with a finger on one hand while

10 A piece of aluminum foil over the magnet and roadbed edge will protect the magnet from paint, glue, and ballast.

11 I laid the flextrack with more construction adhesive, then rolled it to secure it.

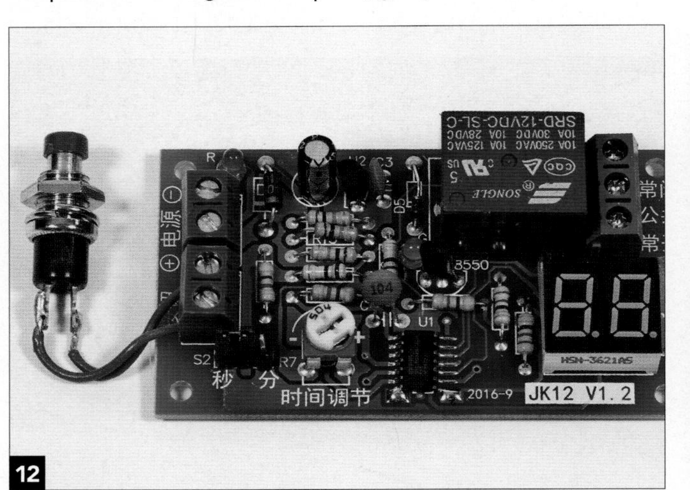

12 This timer circuit will energize the electromagnet for a preset time, both freeing operators' hands and protecting the unit.

13 This large, smooth momentary contact pushbutton switch from All Electronics won't get snagged by loose clothing.

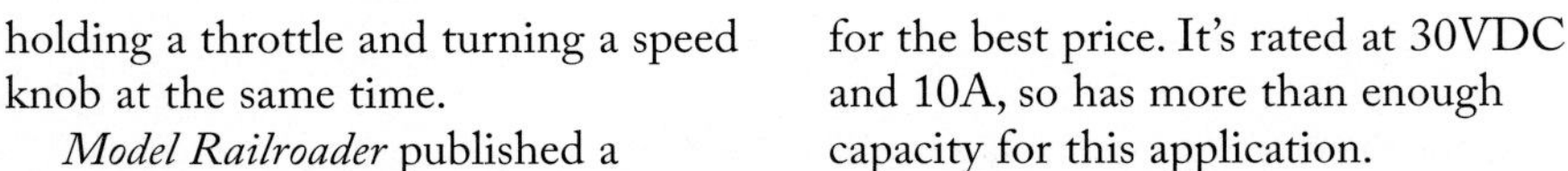

holding a throttle and turning a speed knob at the same time.

Model Railroader published a couple of articles (November 2011 and November 2015) showing circuits that allow hands-free operation of Kadee electromagnets. The basic idea is to use a pushbutton to activate the electromagnet, which then will stay on for about 20 seconds. This gives crews time to uncouple a car or locomotive without having to hold down a button at the same time.

There are also numerous circuits available on the Internet that use similar relay-based designs controlled by an LM555 timer integrated circuit. To save time and provide more options I purchased a circuit, **12**, from a supplier on eBay. A number of sellers offer the same circuits, so shop around for the best price. It's rated at 30VDC and 10A, so has more than enough capacity for this application.

The device is triggered by a pushbutton which turns on a relay activating the load, in this case the electromagnet. The relay remains on for a preset length of time—mine allowed a time range of 1-99 seconds or 1-99 minutes. I set mine for 20 seconds.

I used one of these timers for each electromagnet. However, if you want to save a few dollars, a multiple-position rotary switch lets you install just one circuit board and route power to the electromagnet you want to turn on. The limitation with this approach is that it is a two-step procedure and you can only operate one electromagnet at a time. A large, smooth pushbutton switch on the fascia makes it easy for crews to activate the circuit and lessens the chance of it getting accidentally bumped or snagged by clothing. Mine is from All Electronics, **13**.

You also need a way to let your train crews know where the electromagnet is buried under the rails. You can paint one or more ties over the centerline of the electromagnet, but that looks unprototypical to me. Some use visual markers such as a length of rusty rail or pile of ties.

My solution is a short white marker post at the mid-point of the electromagnet, **1**. I cut these from wooden ties, dip them in white paint, weather them with some diluted India ink, and insert them into a hole punched into the edge of the ballast. I also install the pushbutton in the fascia directly in front of the electromagnet.

CHAPTER TEN

Adding and wiring a lift-out bridge

Around-the-wall layout designs have great advantages, but they often run into obstacles such as doorways. Some have resorted to duck-under arrangements to span these openings, but another popular option is a hinged bridge or lift-out section that be moved out of the way for passage.

Lift-out sections are a great way to span doorways and access areas, as on my HO scale Piedmont Southern layout. Keeping lift-outs aligned properly will ensure smooth operations, and wiring them to kill power to adjoining track sections when removed will protect your trains from falls.

2 The alignment saddles are made from 1x3 poplar. Make sure the holes for the T-nuts are perpendicular.

3 Round-head carriage bolts serve as side guides. Furniture glides provide a level surface for the base.

4 After attaching the alignment saddles to 4"x7" poplar mounting plates, screw the finished assemblies to the edge of the layout.

5 A 38" length of 1x6, ripped to a width of 4", forms the bridge. The thin vertical sides add rigidity and protect rolling stock in case of a derailment.

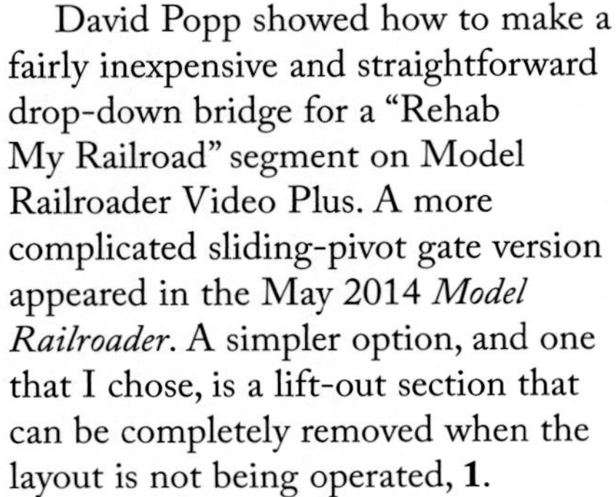

David Popp showed how to make a fairly inexpensive and straightforward drop-down bridge for a "Rehab My Railroad" segment on Model Railroader Video Plus. A more complicated sliding-pivot gate version appeared in the May 2014 *Model Railroader*. A simpler option, and one that I chose, is a lift-out section that can be completely removed when the layout is not being operated, **1**.

One challenge of almost every design I've seen is that lift-outs can be difficult to initially level and adjust. They also are subject to future alignment problems due to expansion and contraction of benchwork materials or movement of the layout benchwork that supports them. I recently learned a new approach from frequent *Model Railroader* contributor and custom layout builder Lance Mindheim (www.lancemindheim.com). His lift-out design uses built-in carriage bolts to adjust the bridge both horizontally and vertically, allowing precise alignment at any time during and after construction. With his approval I've incorporated this aspect of his design into the one I will show here.

Saddles

The heart of this design is what Lance calls alignment saddles. These are placed at the ends of the track on each side of the desired lift-out bridge and allow vertical and horizontal adjustments. I made these of pieces of 1x2 (finished dimensions ¾"x1½") poplar in an "U" arrangement, **2**. The crosspiece of the "U" serves as the bridge support and the sides are for alignment. Your dimensions will be dependent upon the dimensions of the lift-out itself. To allow for the width of the bridge and movement of the adjustment screws, I made my crosspiece 5½" long and the uprights 2¼" with an assembled width of 7".

I drilled holes for two T-nuts in the base and one on each side, **3**, then inserted ¼"x2" carriage bolts into the T-nuts. Take my advice and install the T-nuts into the side pieces before assembling the alignment saddles—it's difficult to hammer them into place once they are assembled. The rounded heads of the side carriage bolts guide the lift-out section smoothly into the saddle.

6 Rerailer track sections are installed flush with the ends of the bridge and the layout.

7 Track nails (in holes drilled into the rerailers) provide additional stability with the adhesive.

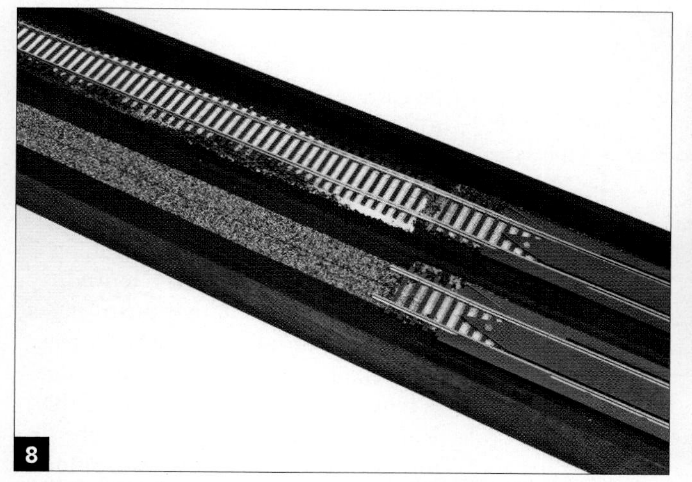

8 After the rerailers are in place, cut and fit sections of flextrack and secure them with Liquid Nails for Projects.

9 Solder 20-gauge feeder wires to each rail near both ends of the bridge.

I used screw-mount furniture glides instead of standard carriage bolts on the bottom. These are 1" in diameter and flat, providing a more stable base than carriage bolt heads, yet they can be screwed in and out to provide height adjustments just like the carriage bolts. (Table bases or table feet will also work.) You can find these in furniture-making catalogs and of course on eBay and Amazon. Also, if the alignment saddle is in an exposed position you can use shorter bolts so the ends don't extend out and snag clothing.

After gluing and nailing the alignment saddles together I attached each to a mounting plate made from a 4"x7" rectangle of poplar (you can use thin plywood as well), using wood screws. I then screwed this to the edge of the layout, **4**.

Bridge

My lift-out is a double-track section. The construction is simple: a 38" length of 1x6 poplar that I ripped on a table saw to 4" wide. A single-track line could use a 1x4 or 1x3 without adjusting. I added vertical sides using ¼" thick, 1½"-wide poplar, **5** (any thin plywood or board will work). The edge pieces prevent trains from falling off in case of derailments on the bridge. They also strengthen the bridge to prevent sagging.

I added cork roadbed to the bridge using Liquid Nails for Projects construction adhesive and rolled this with a wallpaper roller for good adhesion, making sure the track spacing matched the adjoining main line. I then applied 1"-wide blue masking tape down the center of each strip of cork and spray-painted the bridge black so it would stand out in the door opening. The color, of course, is up to you—I may yet end up adding white or yellow barricade stripes to mine as a warning!

Here's where the adjustable saddles prove their worth. As you place the lift-out into the saddles, adjust both the side guides and base glides until the roadbed on the lift-out is level with the roadbed on the adjoining track and the centerlines match as well.

My track is glued in place with Liquid Nails for Projects. I installed Atlas rerailers at each end of the bridge and also on the approach tracks, **6**. I installed the rerailers flush with the ends of the bridge and the edge of the layout, **7**. Note that the rails are removed from the free ends of the

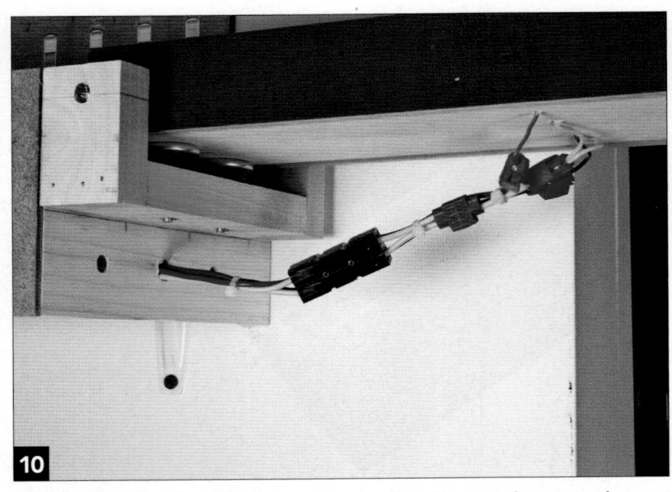

The bridge feeder wires are attached to the track power bus using Anderson Powerpole polarized connectors.

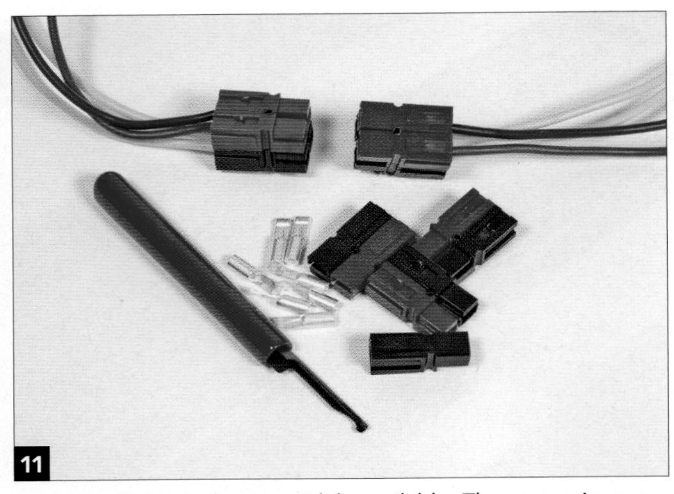

Anderson Powerpoles are widely available. They come in many sizes and allow making polarized connectors by joining the red and black modular units in any combination needed.

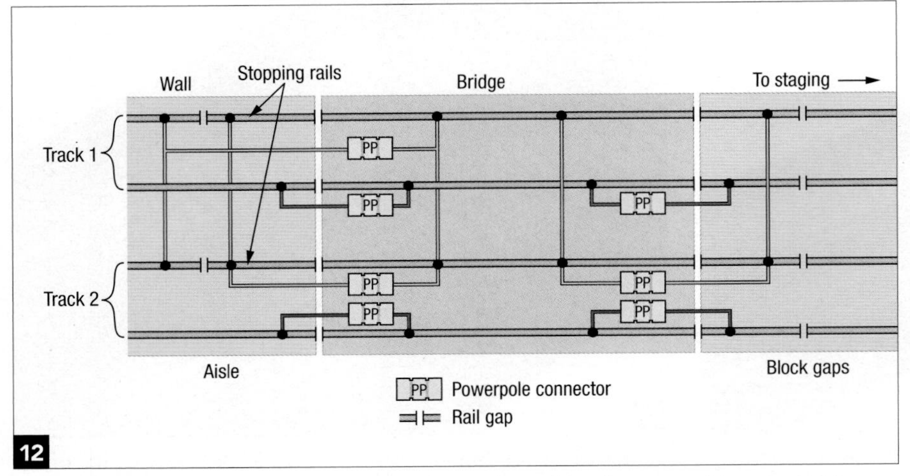

I wired the bridge so that power to the last 2 feet of track approaching the bridge is shut off when the bridge is removed. Power is supplied to the bridge through connections on the left and then back to the rails through the wires. On the right-hand side, power flows from the bridge rails to the approach rails up to the block gaps. When the wires are disconnected, power to the approach rails is killed.

rerailers so that when the bridge is in position the plastic parts of the rerailers almost touch. This lessens the chances of popping the rails from the ties when placing and removing the bridge.

As an added measure of security I drove a couple track nails into holes drilled in the rerailers. Using a flat file I chamfered the inside edges of the rails at the joints to further lessen the chances of derailments. After installing the rerailer tracks I cut and fit sections of flextrack on the bridge, **8**.

Wiring

I soldered 20-gauge solid feeder wires to the rails near each end of the bridge, **9**, and left the wires long enough to reach the edge of the layout plus a little extra for adjustments. I used Anderson Powerpoles to create polarized connectors which I attached to the feeder wires from the layout and the bridge, **10**. Double-check the polarity when wiring the connections!

These modular connectors come in various sizes but the PP30 seems the best choice for most model railroad applications, **11**. I prefer these over Cinch Jones and similar connectors since they have very low electrical resistance. They allow operators to easily disconnect and reconnect the power feed to the bridge while guaranteeing that polarity will always be correct. I recommend getting a variety of them—you'll find them extremely handy for many wiring applications on any model railroad.

To prevent locomotives from accidentally running into the gaping chasm when the bridge is removed, I wired the bridge so that the track power is interrupted to the last 2 feet of track on each side when the bridge is removed. The wiring circuit for this is shown in **12**. It's easy to do—the first impulse is to wire the lift-out section directly to the track bus, but I instead wired one of the approach tracks to the bridge.

To do this I cut a gap in one rail of each approach track 2 feet from the edge. I added a feeder which I connected to the same rails on the bridge. I then ran a wire from the track power buses to the bridge rails. When the bridge is in place and the wires are connected, power flows from the bridge to the isolated rails and completes the circuit. As soon as the connector is uncoupled, the power is killed to this last 2 feet of isolated track. This method eliminates the need for separate switches to kill power when the bridge is removed.

You can adapt these methods to lift-outs and bridges of any size and in any scale, and adjust the design to suit your layout. Thanks again to Lance Mindheim for sharing his ideas with me.

CHAPTER ELEVEN

DC controls for switch machines

Different situations call for different solutions and that holds true for turnout controls, **1**. A lot of folks in my area have opted for using either turnouts with built-in springs like those made by Micro Engineering and Peco, **2**, or simple Caboose Industries ground-throw turnout controls, **3**. All of these allow operators to align turnout points with a flip of a finger, plus they are inexpensive options.

Tortoise switch machines operated by toggle switches on the layout fascia or control panels allow remote operation and simplify controlling turnouts along complex track configurations like this one on my HO layout.

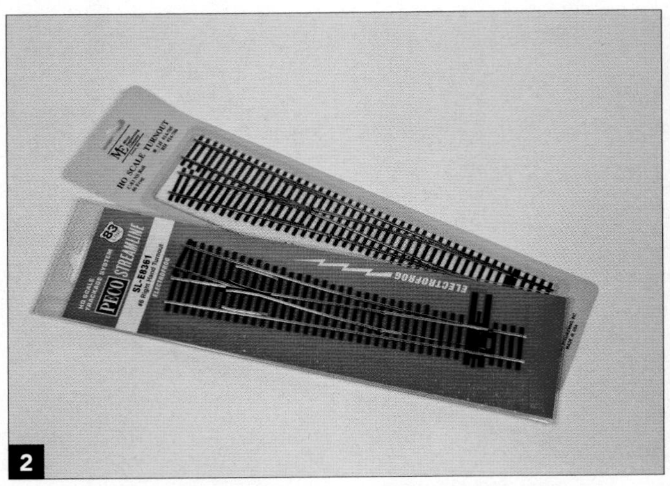

Turnouts with built-in springs like those made by Micro Engineering and Peco are an inexpensive option for aligning turnouts, "snapping" the points into position.

Caboose Industries ground throws work well, are inexpensive, and are easy to install, but require reaching into the layout to control.

Stall-motor switch machines like Circuitron's Tortoise and Smail (a Tortoise with a built-in DCC accessory decoder) operate smoothly and quietly.

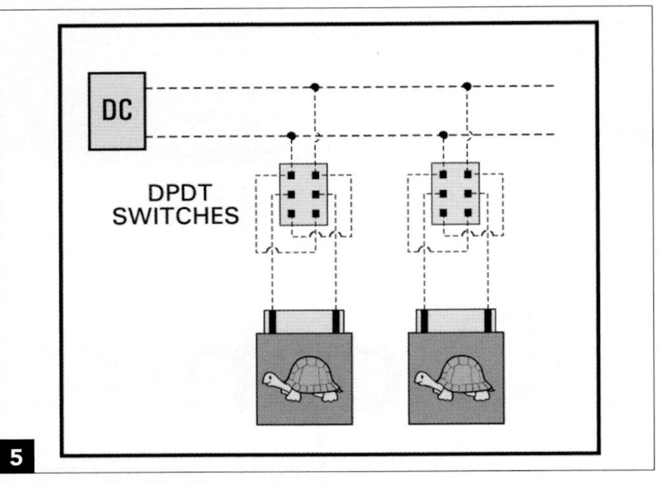

The simplest method for powering a Tortoise employs a 12VDC power supply with a double-pole, double-throw (DPDT) switch to control polarity. *Courtesy Circuitron*

The problem with these approaches is that operators have to reach into scenes on the layout to align turnout points. On an operation-based layout, I've found this often results in inadvertent damage to scenery, structures, locomotives, rolling stock, and anything else that gets in the way. A friend who uses manual controls told me he has to spend a day after each operating session fixing all the things operators break.

This is one reason why many modelers have turned to electric switch machines. Solenoid-based machines (the kind that "snap" switch points into place) have been around since the hobby's early days. By the 1970s, slow-motion switch machines powered by small electric motors were readily available. Circuitron's Tortoise (and the decoder-equipped Smail), **4**, are popular choices. Other manufacturers also make similar machines, but a nice feature of the Tortoise is its multiple electrical contacts that can be used to power indicator lights and perform other functions.

The slow-motion motors are always on. They simply stall once they move the points the proper direction. As the name implies, they move switch points slowly (without the violent "snap") and hold points firmly to their stock rails. The motors draw very little current, so stalling does not damage them.

Best of all, they allow us to align turnouts without poking our hands and fingers into scenes. The downside is they are more expensive than manual options, and they require some way to power and control them. Here we'll look at several basic ways to power the popular Tortoise machines and how to use toggle switches to operate them.

Wiring

Tortoises require a maximum of 12VDC and draw only 15-16mA when fully stalled. At lower voltage they will operate slower and run quieter.

There are several ways to power them. Probably the simplest method is a 12VDC power supply with a double-pole, double-throw (DPDT) switch to control polarity, **5**. With this method, only two wires are required for the

Wiring DPDT switches in a reversing pattern allows swapping polarity to the Tortoise motor.

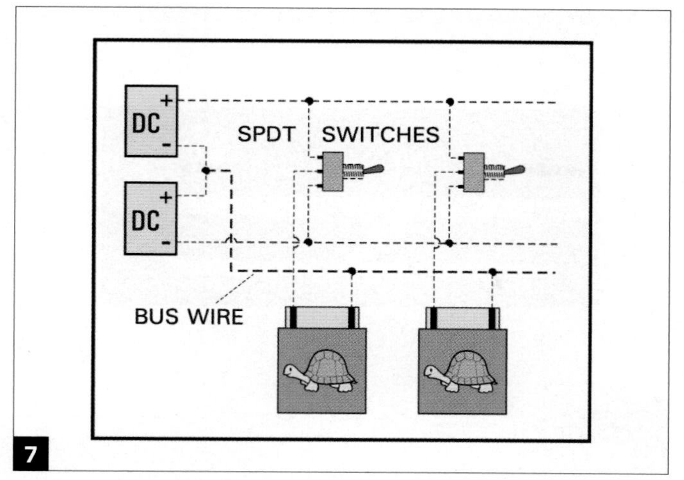

Another method requires two DC power supplies of the same rating, allowing SPDT switches to control polarity. *Courtesy Circuitron*

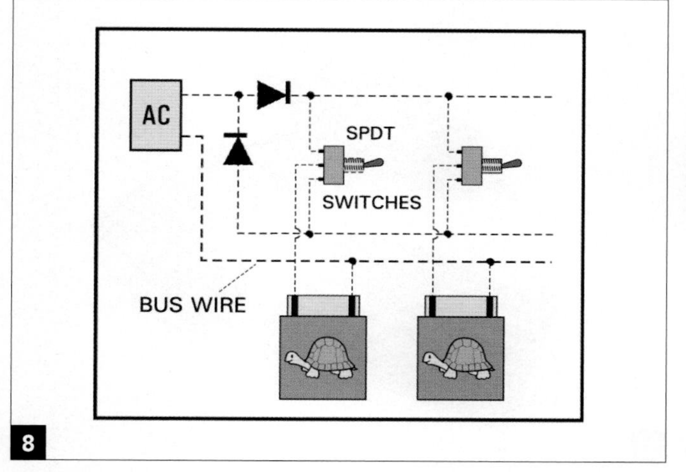

Another option is an AC power supply with one pole routed through a pair of diodes. *Courtesy Circuitron*

To simplify installation I like to pre-install the wires on the Tortoises and use quick-connects for the final connection to the power bus.

power bus. However, it does require using more-expensive double-pole switches and wiring each in a reversing pattern, **6**. Whenever the switch is thrown the polarity will reverse and the motor will change direction.

The second method requires two DC power supplies of the same rating, but allows single-pole, double-throw (SPDT) switches, **7**, with no additional switch wiring. With this method, one positive and one negative terminal of each power supply are wired together and connected to a motor contact on the Tortoise. The other positive and negative terminal on each power supply are then routed through the SPDT switch and connected to the other motor contact. Throwing the switch reverses the polarity and changes motor direction. Although the SPDT switches are cheaper than DPDT ones, the added complexity and cost of two power supplies, along with the need for three bus wires, are a downside.

A third method employs an AC power supply with one pole routed through a pair of diodes wired in reverse polarity to create half-wave DC, **8**. Like the second method it uses SPDT switches and three bus wires connected similarly. However because it uses half-wave DC, a larger (14-16VAC) power supply is required.

Because each Tortoise only requires about 15-16 mA, you can power about 60 of them with a 1A power supply.

After you install each switch motor, test it with your power supply to determine which wire to connect to the motor contacts in order to synchronize it with your SPDT or DPDT control switch. To simplify installation I pre-install the wires on the Tortoises and use quick-connects, **9**, for the final connections—this makes it easy to swap wires and match polarity. It also means I don't have to make solder connections to the circuit board under the layout. Another option is purchasing card-edge connector strips with screw terminals—these slide on and off of the Tortoise terminal card.

Control panels

Where should the SPDT or DPDT switches be mounted? You have a few

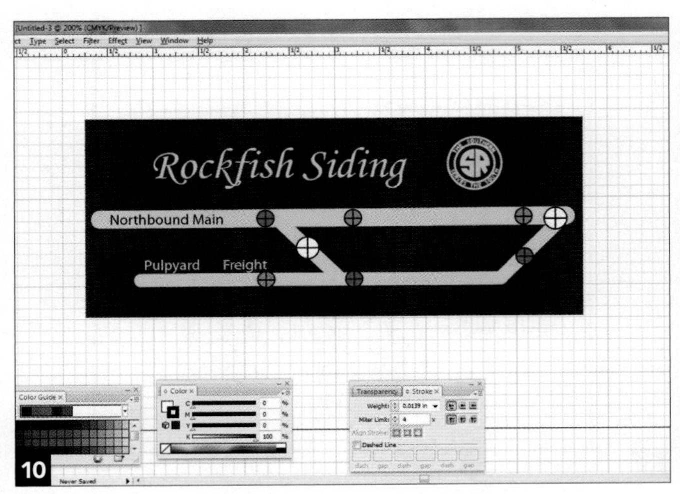

If there are two or three turnouts located together, a computer-generated track diagram helps identify the turnouts being controlled.

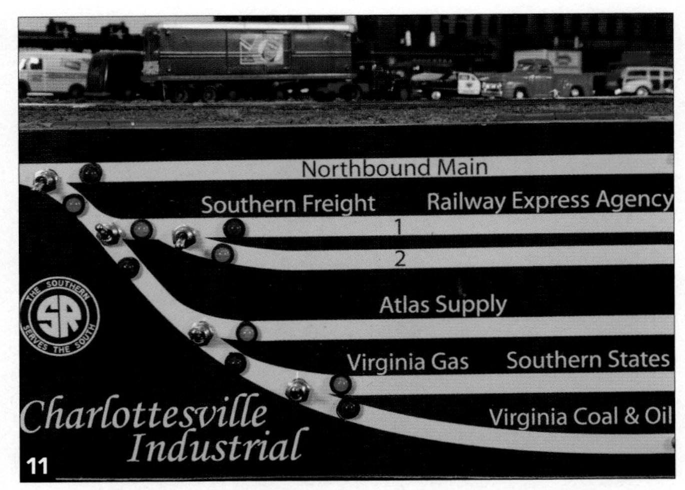

11. For complex trackwork, separate control panels with detailed diagrams simplify operations.

I build control panels with a 1 x 1 poplar frame and attach a face of thin plywood or hardboard.

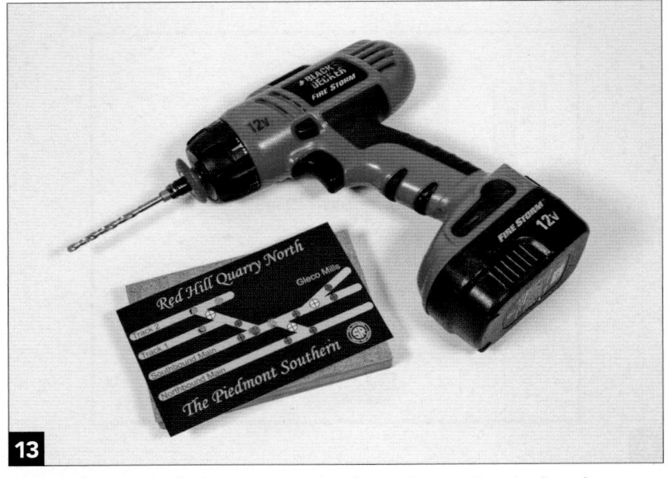

Place the track diagram over the board, punch a hole where each switch and LED goes, then remove the diagram and drill the mounting holes.

options. Some modelers install them in the fascia directly in front of the turnouts they control. If there are two or three turnouts in the same location, consider adding a track diagram, **10**, attached directly to the fascia with each toggle switch mounted on the diagram at turnout it controls. For protection these diagrams can be laminated and glued to the fascia before installing the switches.

More-complex trackwork requires a little more care. For clusters of more than two or three turnouts, I opt for building a larger control panel with a detailed diagram of the track and all involved turnouts, **11**. For these I prefer one of two similar methods. The method I use is to build a frame of 1 x 1 pine strip and attach a face of either thin plywood or hardboard, **12**. I create a track diagram using a computer graphics program, punch a hole where each switch and LED goes, and place the diagram on the face of the control panel. I then mark the locations of all the switches using the holes as a pattern, remove the diagram, and drill the proper size hole for the switches and LEDs, **13**.

Adding a piece of ⅛" clear acrylic over the track diagram is a nice touch. I place it on the face, mark the locations of the switches, then drill the holes, including a set at the four corners to serve as screw holes. Finally I overlay the track diagram with the acrylic on the panel and install the switches. The switches I had on hand didn't have a tall enough collar to extend through both the hardboard face and acrylic sheet, so I had to cut out the area of hardboard around the switches and just mount them to the acrylic, **14**.

Another option I plan to try is to laminate the printed diagram and install it directly on the hardboard, eliminating the clear acrylic. This would be easier to build, reduce the cost of each control panel, and make the panel thin enough for mounting switches.

Another useful addition to these control panels are LEDs installed on the diagrams to show which leg of a turnout is selected, **15**. Following convention, I use green LEDs for the

My toggle switches didn't have tall-enough collars to extend through both the hardboard face and acrylic sheet, so I cut out the area of hardboard and just mounted them to the acrylic.

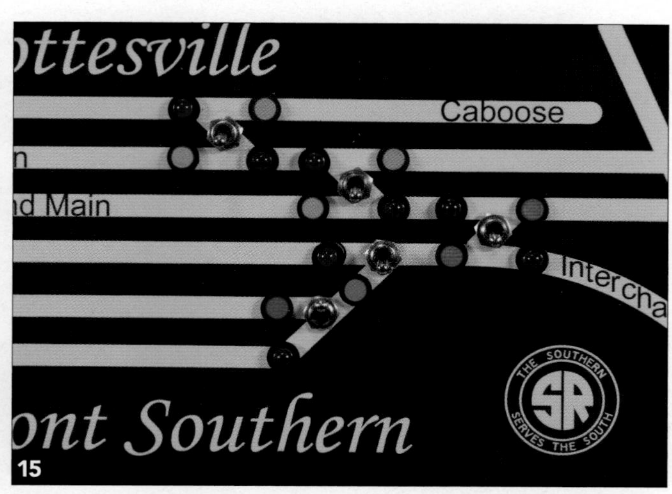

LEDs installed on the panel diagrams show which leg of each turnout is selected.

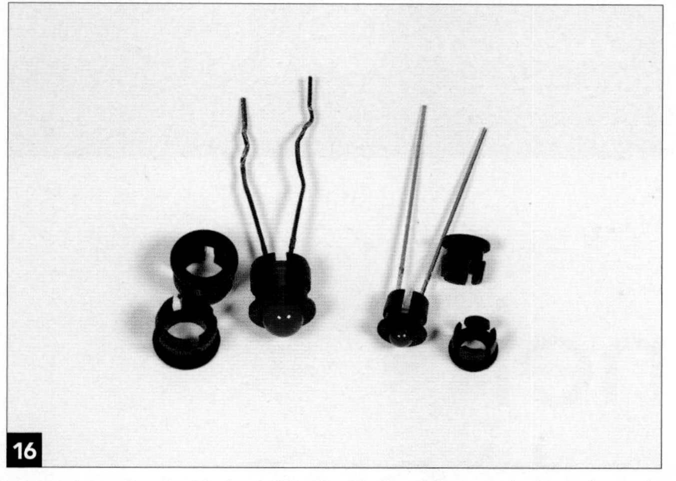

Mounting clips hold the LEDs firmly in place on the panels and provide a neat appearance.

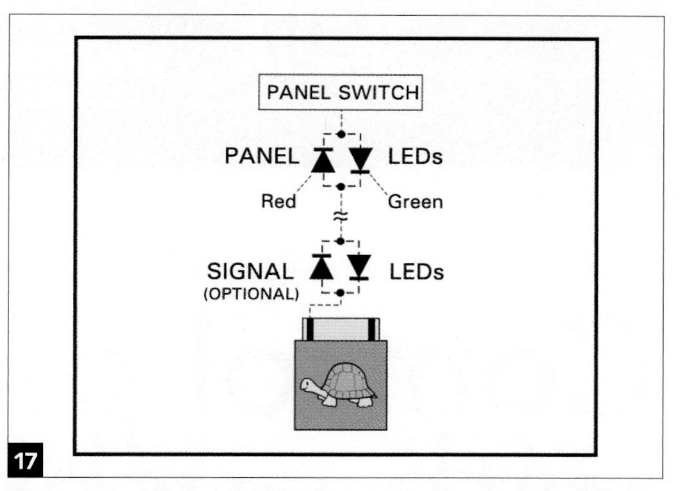

Wiring LEDs for directional indications is a matter of installing them along one of the wires powering the Tortoise. *Courtesy Circuitron*

normal direction of travel and red for when the turnout is aligned for the diverging route. Even if one or more of your engineers is red-green color blind, the fact that the LEDs are lit makes the direction of travel obvious. Some modelers use LEDs of the same color or even install bicolor LEDs, but I prefer the red-green arrangement as it is commonly used in the hobby and real railroading for designating turnout positions.

Installing LEDs is simple using mounting clips available from All Electronics and others, **16**. These are available for both conventional 3mm and 5mm round LEDs, and they fit on the track diagram in 3⁄16" and 1⁄4" holes, respectively. These hold the LEDs firmly in place and give the panel a neat appearance.

Wiring the LEDs is simple: They can be installed along one of the wires powering the Tortoise, **17**. Note in the diagram the orientation of the LEDs uses the standard symbol for a diode, with the perpendicular line indicating the negative leg. On most LEDs one of the "legs" is longer, indicating the positive connection. Another indicator is the flat spot molded into the plastic housing on the negative side.

I install the red and green LED pairs in the panel, then twist and solder the negative and positive legs together. One power feed wire is then soldered to one of the joined legs; another wire soldered to the other pair goes on to the Tortoise. The second power feed wire goes directly to the Tortoise. These are then connected to solder pads one and eight on the Tortoise circuit board.

Depending on the polarity of the wire, the red or green LED will illuminate when the panel switch is thrown to change the direction of the turnout. After installing a few of these you'll get a feel for the relationship of the turnout position and how you wire the LEDs—you can't destroy them by reverse wiring.

This arrangement works because LEDs will light with the 15 to 16mA current that the Tortoises require. Each LED will drop the voltage by about 2V, so you can expect the turnouts to operate a little slower.

CHAPTER TWELVE

Control panel with pushbuttons

A control panel with pushbuttons and LEDs to indicate turnout alignment makes it easy for train crews to quickly select routes through complex trackage.

The previous chapter showed how to build control panels and use toggle switches to control switch machines. This chapter explains a simple way to control turnouts using Digital Command Control (DCC) accessory decoders and pushbutton switches on a panel, **1**. Pushbutton switches make it easier for operators to control turnouts and are simple to install.

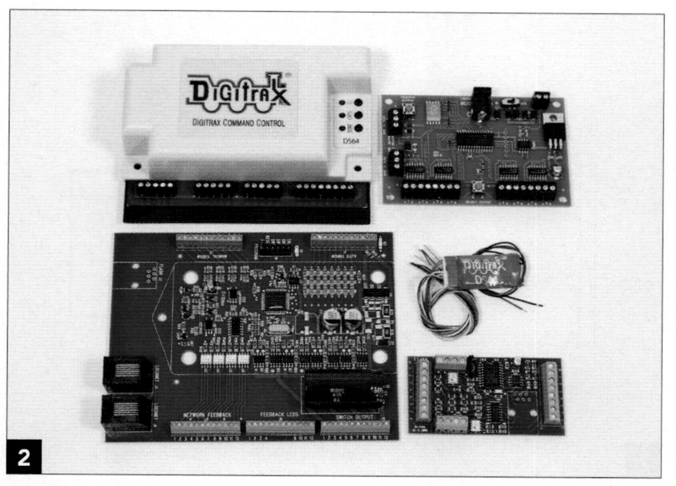

2

Accessory decoders come in a variety of shapes and sizes. Many control multiple switch machines, and some have up to eight outputs.

3

The Circuitron Smail (left) is a Tortoise with a built-in accessory decoder. The DCC Specialties Hare (center) and the NCE Switch-It Mk2 (right) decoders mount directly on the Tortoise.

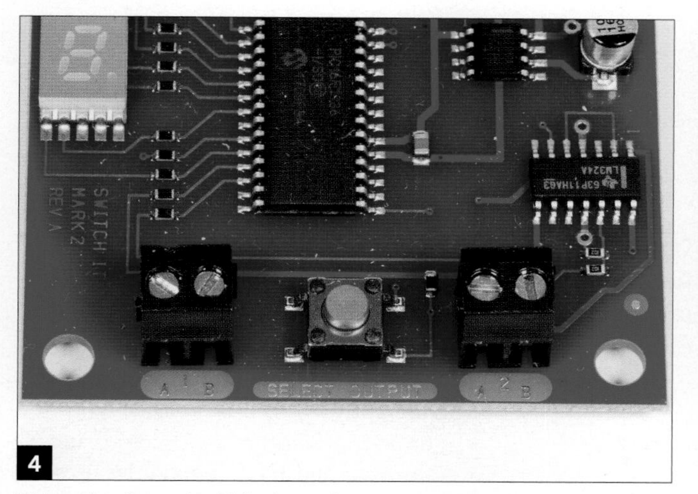

4

This pair of terminal blocks with two screws each (at the front edge of the board) make it easy to connect the switch machine motor leads to the Switch-It.

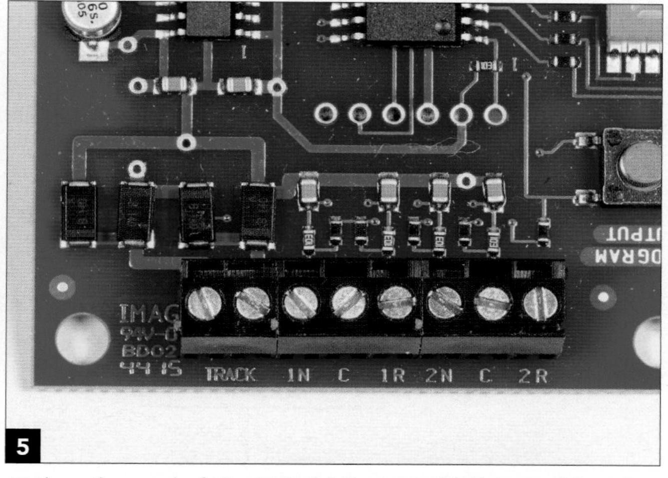

5

At the other end of the Switch-It is a terminal block with eight screws for connecting power feeds and control switches.

Let's start with a look at a few different accessory decoders, which are great for those out-of-the-way places on your layout that may only have a couple turnouts to be controlled. We'll then move to a slightly more complex situation with multiple turnouts using a larger accessory decoder.

Accessory decoders, **2**, come in a variety of sizes and capabilities with anywhere from one to eight outputs. They are similar to DCC mobile decoders in that each of its outputs is assigned a unique address. Also like mobile decoders, commands can be sent specifically to each accessory decoder address to control switch machines, lights, motors, and just about anything that operates electrically.

More importantly, in addition to being able to control accessory decoders using your throttle or a computer, most can also be locally controlled using pushbutton or toggle switches. In this case we'll use the decoder outputs to control and power Tortoise switch machines using pushbutton switches on the fascia or a control panel.

At a few locations on my HO scale Piedmont Southern I only have one or two turnouts to control, so fancy programming capability and a complicated control panel are not required. Instead Circuitron now offers a version of the Tortoise, the Smail, with a built-in accessory decoder, **3**. Just install it like you would a Tortoise and hook it up to your track power bus.

Another simple solution, especially if you already have Tortoises on hand (or have them installed), is a clip-on accessory decoder like the DCC Specialties Hare or the NCE Switch-It Mk2. The Hare literally clips onto the circuit board of the Tortoise using a card edge connector. The Switch-It is small enough to be attached to a Tortoise using double-sided foam tape or hot glue and can control a pair of switch machines, making it perfect for controlling a pair of turnouts forming a crossover. Both can be operated with a throttle or switches mounted on the fascia or a control panel as in Chapter 11. The difference with the Switch-It is that it can control two Tortoises.

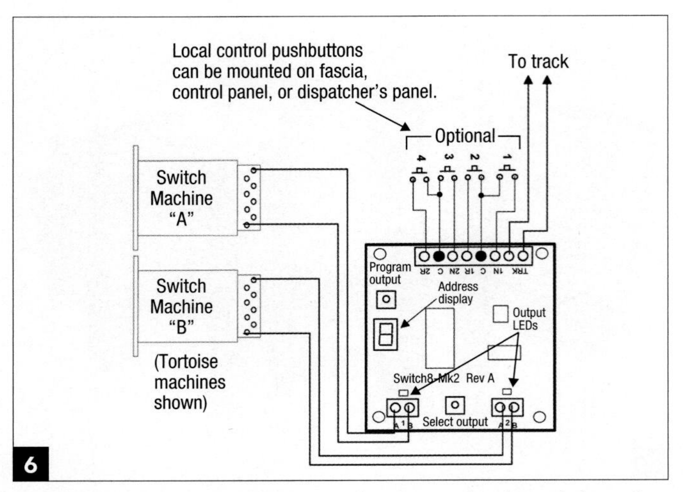

6

The first two screw positions are for power feeds and the other six screw positions are for the normal and reversed pushbutton or toggle switches (1N, 1R, 2N, 2R). The position labeled "C" is the common connection for each switch. *Courtesy NCE*

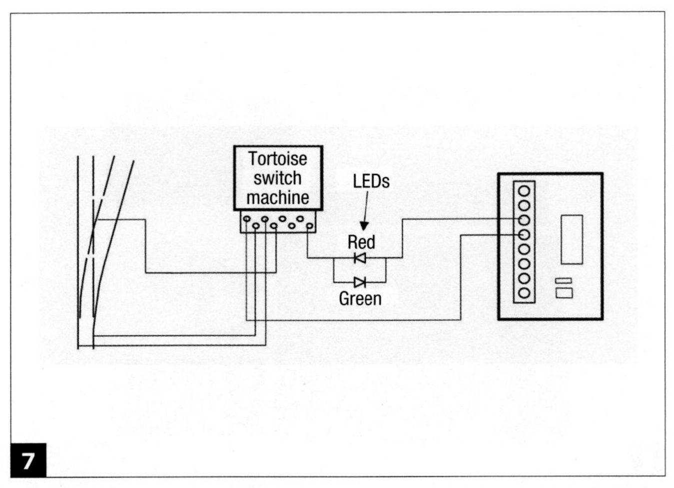

7

You can wire a pair of LEDs into one lead to the Tortoise motor to display directional lighting on a control panel or lineside signal. *Courtesy NCE*

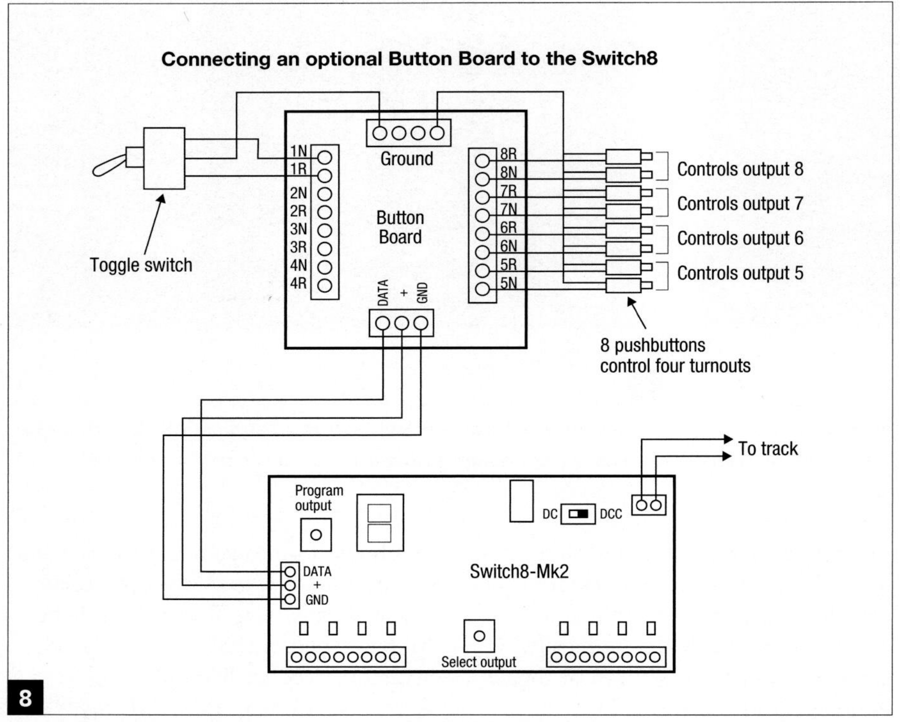

8

Only three wires are required to connect the Button Board to the Switch8. Either toggles or pushbuttons can be connected to the Button Board.

Unless you install additional hardware that allows you to operate two turnouts off one Tortoise switch motor you'll need two of them for each crossover. However, the outputs of the Switch-It are powerful enough that you should be able to operate both turnouts used for a crossover using one output. This also simplifies the wiring and programming.

Let's look at how the Switch-It is wired to these two Tortoises. On one end of the Switch-It is a pair of terminal blocks with two screws each, **4**. The wires from the motor contacts on the Tortoises are inserted into the respective output slots and the screws tightened—no soldering is required.

At the other end of the Switch-It is a terminal block with eight screws, **5**. The first two screw positions are for feeders from the DCC track power bus—these provide power for operating the Tortoises as well as the DCC commands for the accessory decoder. Next in line are the screw positions for the normal and reversed pushbutton or toggle switches labelled 1N, 1R, 2N, 2R respectively. (Different manufacturers refer to turnout routes differently. NCE uses "normal" and "reversed," Digitrax uses "closed" and "thrown," and DCC Specialties uses "clear" and "thrown.") Between each pair of these contacts is a common connection labelled C.

With the default settings, two pushbuttons are required to control each route through each turnout. One pushbutton is connected to the N and C terminals and the other to the R and C terminals for each output, **6**. When the NC pushbutton is pushed the straight route is triggered; the RC pushbutton triggers the diverging route.

You can also simplify this so that a single pushbutton controls each output. By programming the decoder's configuration variable (CV) 548 to a value of "1," the outputs on the Switch-It are set to toggle mode and when in toggle mode both outputs are affected. This means that each time the button is pushed it changes the route through the turnout (it doesn't matter whether the pushbutton is

NCE's Switch8 (right) and Button Board combination makes it easy to control up to eight switch machines with pushbuttons.

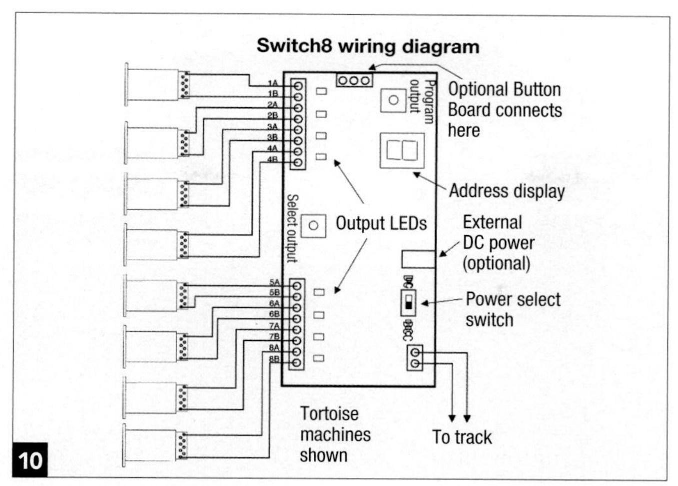

Screw terminal blocks make connecting wires from the Tortoises to the Switch8 quick and easy.

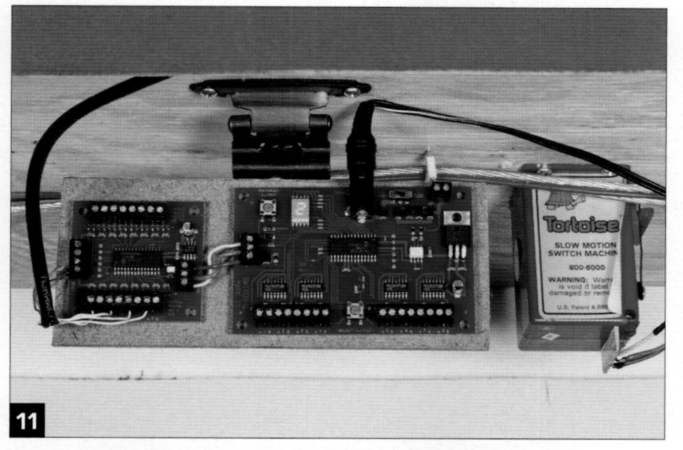

I mounted the Switch8 and Button Board to a piece of hardboard under the layout on a spring-loaded cabinet hinge.

The Switch8 can be powered with a 12VDC power supply connected to the board at the front barrel socket. Be sure to set the slide switch for DC instead of DCC. The DCC power bus connection is to the left of the DC/DCC selector switch.

wired in the NC or RC configuration). Pushbuttons must be the normally open, momentary-contact type. Toggle switches can also be used.

You can wire a pair of LEDs in one wire to the Tortoise motor for directional lighting on a control panel, **7**, as shown in Chapter 11. If after the wires are connected and the Switch-It addresses are programmed the turnout directions are reversed, simply swap the wires at the output screw terminals.

NCE provides excellent instructions on programming the Switch-It using various DCC systems, but in most cases all you need to set are the two output addresses. For a simple setup like this I like to install the pushbutton directly on the fascia in front of the turnouts the Switch-It controls.

For yards and other areas with a lot of turnouts, I prefer the NCE Switch8 and Button Board combination, **8**, **9**. As the name implies, the Switch8 can control eight switch machines with pushbuttons, toggle switches, throttles, command station, or computer commands. Connecting the Button Board to the Switch8 requires only three wires and it has screw terminals for connecting either toggle switches or pushbuttons.

Connecting the Tortoises to the Switch8 is simplified with screw terminal blocks, **10**, which also make it quick and easy to switch wires if the polarity to the Tortoise needs to be changed. The Switch8 and Button Board can be separated by as much as 10 feet and the pushbuttons can be located as far as 20 feet from the Button Board. However, for runs longer than 36" the wires connecting them should be twisted pairs. Another option is CAT5 cable, which has four color-coded twisted pairs.

I attached the Switch8 and Button Board to a piece of hardboard suspended under the layout with a spring-loaded cabinet hinge, **11**. This allows it to swing down for wiring and programming, then swing back up out of the way. I then mounted all those pushbuttons on small control panels attached to the fascia. A DC power connection is provided should you choose to use it instead of DCC power, **12**. I used CAT5 cable to wire the pushbuttons to the Button Board. The flip up panel provides full access, **13**.

13 The color-coded, paired wires in CAT5 cable make it a neat and quick process to connect pushbutton switches to the Button Board. The flip-up panel makes soldering easy.

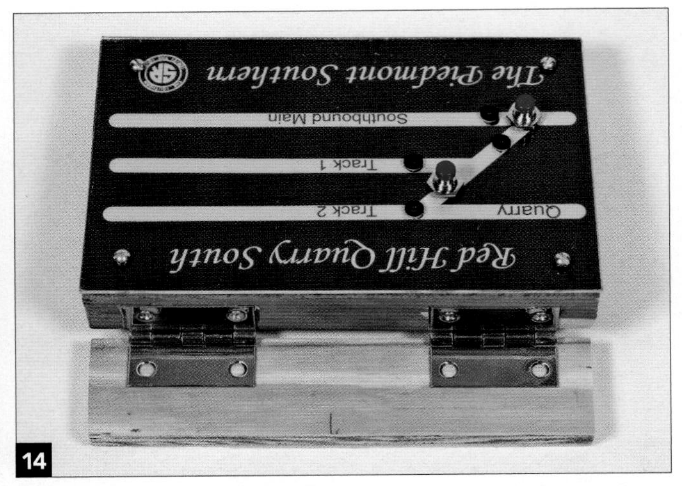

14 Small decorative brass hinges attach the mini-control panels to the layout edge, allowing them to hang vertically on the fascia.

15 I replaced the scenery base foam with a piece of ½" plywood to provide a mounting surface for the panel.

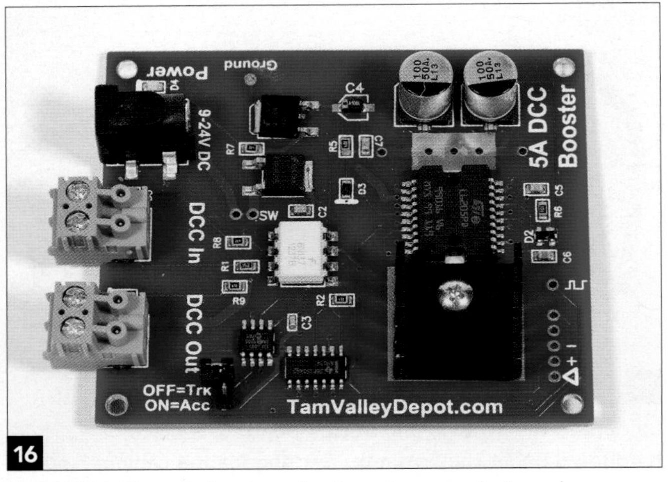

16 Tam Valley Depot's inexpensive booster was designed specifically as a separate power bus for accessory decoders.

Control panel

Chapter 11 described building control panels from strips of molding and hardboard. These hinged panels are smaller but use the same methods.

After building the panel and installing the pushbutton switches and LEDs, I attached small decorative brass hinges at the top, **14**. I then cut out a section of foam atop the layout edge and replaced it with a rectangle of ½" plywood to serve as the base for attaching the hinges, **15**. This allows tilting the panel up to complete wiring or do maintenance. A hole drilled through the fascia behind the panel serves as a pass-through for the wires. The finished control panel makes it easy for train crews to select the correct turnouts with a simple push of a button or two.

Accessory decoders can be powered directly off the track power bus—just hook them up to your main DCC power bus and not only will they receive power, they will also be able to receive commands from throttles, the command station, or a computer.

However, there are a couple downsides to doing this. First, if you have a lot of them, the power they consume will take power away from your locomotives, car lighting, and any other DCC-powered accessories. Also, if a short circuit at a turnout shuts down your boosters there will be no power to cycle that switch and clear the short—a bit of a catch-22. Of course you can use an auxiliary DC power supply as mentioned earlier.

Another option is to use a separate booster as a dedicated power supply for all your accessory decoders. I have a DCC power bus dedicated to powering my accessory decoders. That way they do not create a load on the track power buses. Tam Valley Depot makes an inexpensive booster specifically for this purpose, **16**. It has two screw terminal blocks for making DCC in/out connections and a barrel plug for connecting a 9-24VDC power supply. It can be configured to act as a 3-5A booster for track power or set to be used for powering accessory decoders. While it can supply up to 5A, this is only an instantaneous rating and it is only good for 3A continuously. In accessory mode if the power goes down the Tam Valley Depot booster will stay on for up to five minutes allowing your accessory decoders and anything they control to remain powered.

CHAPTER THIRTEEN

Install a track scale with LED display

I'm always on the lookout for ways to keep yard and local crews busy, so I was pretty excited when I discovered the Boulder Creek Engineering electronic track scale kit a few years ago. Prototype railroads use scales to weigh freight cars, since shipping charges are often based on the weight of a load. Track scales are often located at major yards, and large industries often have their own scales as well.

An empty car pauses for weighing on the scale track at the Charlottesville, Va., yard on my HO Piedmont Southern layout. I installed the Walthers kit, including track and scale house, and then added a Boulder Creek scale simulator.

2

Walthers makes an HO track scale kit that can be used to model both types of scale tracks and structures.

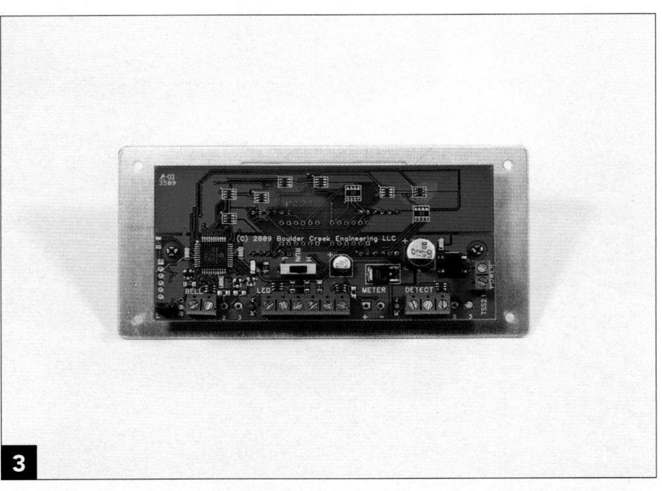
3

Boulder Creek Engineering designed its scale module with the electronics and connectors on the back of the fascia plate.

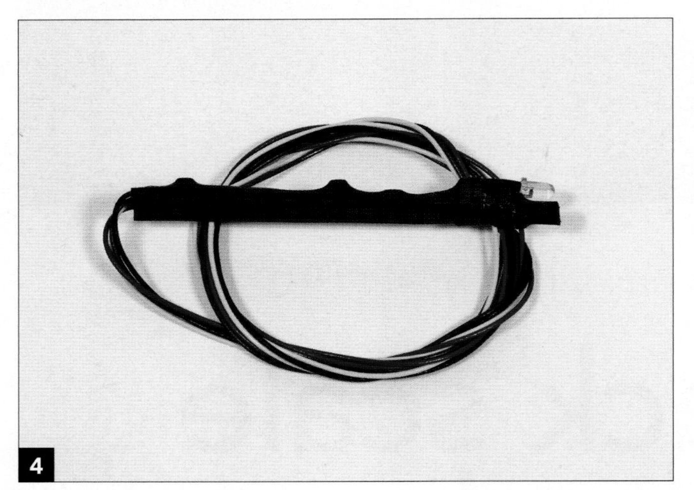
4

The NightScope detector comes as a single unit wrapped in a heat-shrink sleeve. It includes the IR LED, IR phototransistor, and detection electronics.

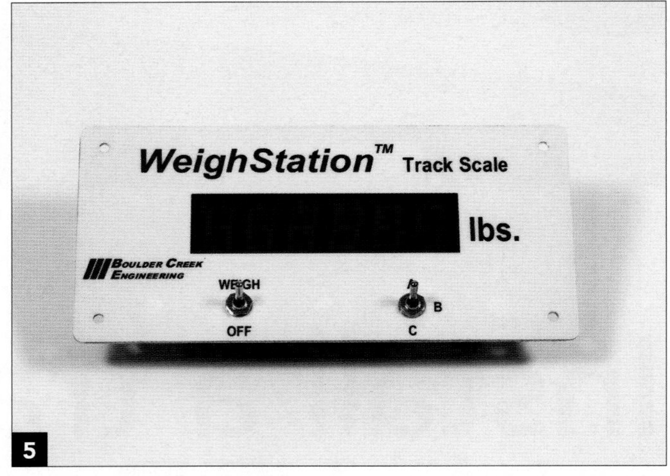

5

The face of the panel includes a large digital display, weigh/off toggle switch, and a three-way weight range selection toggle switch.

There are two basic types of prototype track scales: Weigh-in-motion (or coupled-in-motion), which measures weight (usually the weight of one truck) while a train rolls slowly across the scale, and spot, which requires a car to be placed on the scale and uncoupled. Weigh-in-motion scales didn't become common until the late 1900s but now are used often in large installations.

Spot scales often have two sets of tracks in gantlet style, with one set on the scale itself and one set off the scale to let the locomotive pass while remaining coupled to cars. A scale house is usually located adjacent to the scale track, where the weight is recorded—either by hand or (for modern scales) electronically.

The Boulder Valley kit can be used to model either type of operation, **1**. Walthers makes an HO scale track kit that can be used to model both types of scale tracks and structures, **2**. I installed the Walthers light duty scale in my Charlottesville, Virginia, yard. Let's take a look at what's involved.

You first need to decide which type of scale you want to model. For a spot scale you can add a functioning or dummy gantlet track. Or you can do like I did in Charlottesville and install a sign telling trains crews not to allow locomotives on the scales, forcing them to push cars across and weigh them as they go, then pull the whole string back.

Follow the Walthers instructions for building and painting the scale track, structure, and platform.

Installing the system

Once you have the model built you can add the Boulder Valley electronics, **3**. The system detects the presence of a car by bouncing an infrared beam off the bottom of the car, which is then detected by a built-in infrared phototransistor. The infrared LED and phototransistor come as a single unit wrapped in a heat-shrink sleeve that also includes the detection electronics, **4**. The scale electronics, built into the display unit, produce a random weight for the car on either a digital screen, **5**, or an analog needle meter. Three different weight ranges can be selected using a switch on the display panel.

You can install red, green, and yellow LEDs, **6**, and a buzzer to let crews know when to stop the car and

The red and green LEDs and a buzzer let crews know when to stop the car and when to proceed. The scale displays a random weight for the car.

With the Walthers kits you have to drill a hole or cut a slot in the scale track platform for the detector and drill the mounting holes for the NightScope detector.

Before mounting the display, connect the various wires following instructions. With multiple screw terminals, no soldering is required.

Power up the circuit and display. Make sure everything works properly before screwing the faceplate to the fascia.

when to proceed once the weighing is done. In my experience, once installed and adjusted, the system is reliable and not overly sensitive to stray ambient overhead light.

The first thing to do is install the infrared LED and phototransistor detector. This isn't difficult, requiring only a 1/8" hole for the LED and an 11/64" hole for the phototransistor in the roadbed, **7**.

When locating the sensors there are two options: place them alongside the scale track, 3/16" from the outside of the rail; or center them between the rails of the scale track. I chose the second option since it avoids problems with the detector failing to "see" certain types of cars.

The rounded bottoms of tank cars, for example, may not consistently reflect the infrared beam back down to the phototransistor. Covered and open hoppers with their angled bottoms may have similar problems. With the detector centered you are more likely to get a good signal bounced off the center beam of the car. However, this location comes with its own issue—the beam may bounce off couplers and give a false detection as cars roll overhead. I found that by offsetting the detector about 1/8" instead of placing it dead center you can avoid this problem.

I cut out a rectangle in the fascia in front of the track scale using the template provided in the kit. Next I drilled two 5mm diameter holes in the fascia above the cutout and installed red and green LEDs (resistors are not needed as the circuit board already has them). With the detector and LEDs in place I connected the various wires to the back of the display/control panel including the connections to my 12VDC power bus, **8**. With everything attached I powered it up just as a test before installing it in the fascia, **9**.

The scale has three weight settings. They're adjustable but are preset for loaded cars of 50,000 to 200,000 pounds, empties of 40,000 to 50,000 pounds, and scale test cars of 80,000 pounds. I changed mine to heavy weights for ballast hoppers and pulp racks weighing 190,000-200,000 pounds, medium weights of 140,000-

The Milwaukee Road had a gantlet-style scale track and scale house at its Chestnut Street Yard in Milwaukee in 1975.
Gordon Odegard

170,000 pounds, and empties weighing 40,000-50,000 pounds.

To change the weight ranges, just set the weigh switch on the front of the panel for the range you want to change and then on the back of the unit move the mode switch from Run to L. The unit will display the weight increasing in 10,000-pound steps. When it reaches the minimum weight you want, slide the switch to the H position and it will begin to increase in 10,000-pound steps. When it reaches the maximum weight you want, move the switch back to Run. You can change the other weight ranges in the same manner.

To weigh cars, pull or push a car onto the scale. The green light will go out and the red light will illuminate, telling you to stop. The weight on the display will fluctuate, and once it settles down the green light will come on and a buzzer will sound as a signal to move off the scale and spot a new car. It's up to your crews to change the scale switch to the appropriate weight range for the cars being weighed. As crews weigh the cars they should note them on a report form like the one in **10**.

Because weighing cars can take some time, you may want to modify the process. For example with a spot scale you may want to dispense with the requirement that each car be uncoupled. Some loads didn't require weighing—boxcars of less-than-carload (LCL) freight picked up at a freight house or depot, for example.

This track scale adds a nice bit of animation and operating interest to a layout with minimal work.

Car Weight Report

Location____________________ Date__________

No.	Car no.	Car Initials	Car Type	Weight
1				
2				
3				
4				
5				
6				
7				
8				
9				
10				
11				
12				
13				
14				
15				
16				
17				
18				
19				
20				

10

As crews weigh cars they can write down the weights on a report form like this one.

A working telephone system can be both a great way for the dispatcher to communicate with train crews and a cool piece of nostalgia by using period equipment like this classic scissors-style phone.

CHAPTER FOURTEEN

Install a working telephone system

My HO Piedmont Southern layout is set in 1957. The layout is based on the prototype Southern Ry., which in that period still depended on timetables and train orders for dispatching trains, using telephones for communication. Many large home and club layouts use two-way radio headsets for operations, but I wanted the more-prototypical, nostalgic feel of a telephone system, **1**.

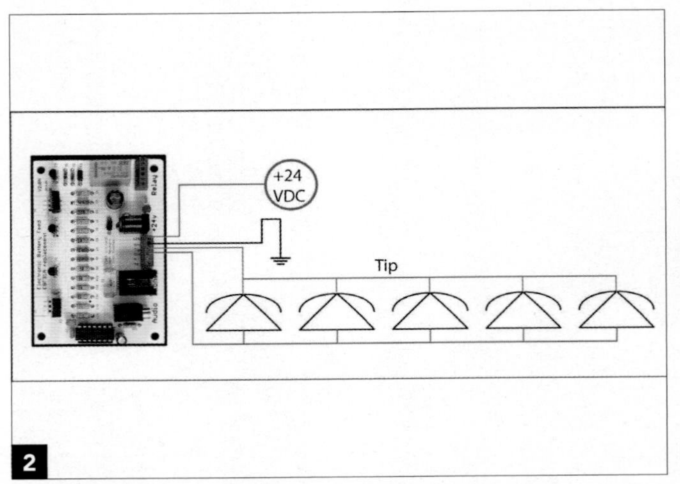

The party-line telephone circuit is essentially the same as that used by telephone companies, with a main power supply and speech network circuit boards providing anti-sidetone and line balancing electronics. *Courtesy Seth Neumann, MRCS*

The EBF31A battery feed circuit board provides a clean power supply and also has connections for the telephone network wires, a relay for optional circuits, and an audio outlet for connecting a loudspeaker.

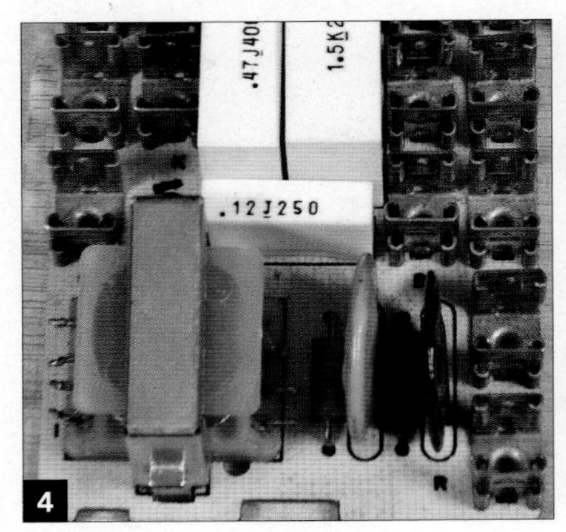

Speech network circuit boards were installed in all telephones. They provide anti-sidetone and line balancing electronics that result in a relatively noise-free telephone network similar to what you experience on a normal land-line phone.

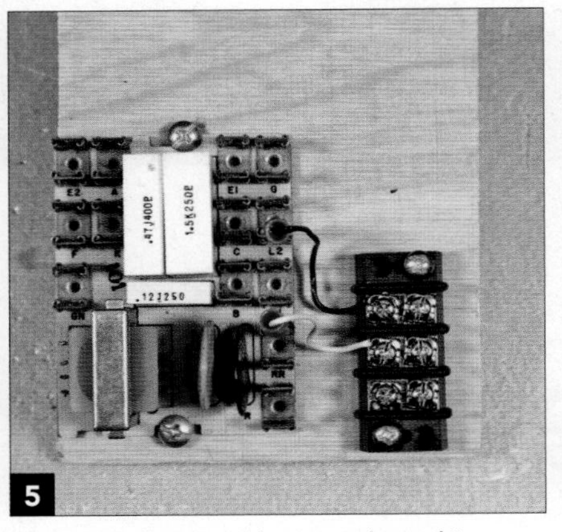

The speech network circuit board is attached to each mounting board using wood screws, placed so the heads grip the edge of the circuit board. The three-position screw terminal at right simplifies attaching and daisy-chaining the main network cable.

Attach the handset cord to the board with a ¼" (or size appropriate for your particular cord) nylon cable clamp.

Among the problems with using radios is that the headsets can be uncomfortable to wear for long sessions. You also hear all other conversations going on, which isn't prototypical unless you're modeling a prototype that actually uses radio for communications.

Other modelers have installed phone systems—Al Westerfield and Don Ball have both shown how to install systems and shared their methods in magazine articles. Seth Neumann, a retired phone company employee, pointed out the problems with these simplified series-wired systems, which can be hampered by electronic noise from transformer-based power supplies, suffer from inconsistent volume, have stray noise on the line from outside sources, and have an old issue called sidetone. Sidetone was common in early telephones, meaning the speaker hears his or her own voice in the receiver. To compensate, they talk lower making it hard for others to hear them.

Another issue with series-wired systems is they can put so much current through the carbon particles in the handsets that they get packed together or fuse over time and fail. Exposure to as little as 100 milliamps of current over a few months can damage the carbon particles.

Seth has given presentations at NMRA conventions recommending alternatives that depend on a more modern telephone network. These incorporate filtered power supplies, properly shielded wiring, and anti-sidetone electronics, which can all be combined with original vintage telephones you can pick up at yard sales and flea markets. Seth and his partners offer electronic components and even old telephones for sale through Model Railroad Control Systems (MRCS,

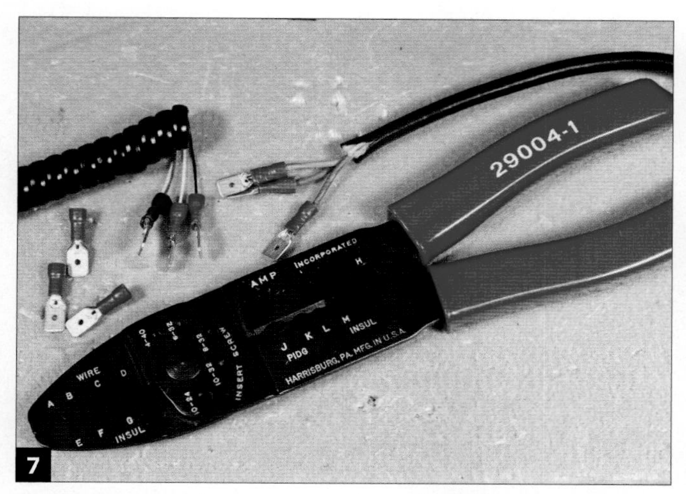

I added male quick-connects to the ends of the wires coming from the F and G style handsets using a crimper tool. I find this much easier than soldering connections.

The ¼" male quick-connects I had were a bit too thick for the slots on the speech networks but a little prying with a small screwdriver tip opened them enough to work.

Dispatchers were responsible for keeping trains on schedule while maintaining safe distances between them. This required regular communication with agents in stations along the line (here typing a train order) using either a telegraph or telephone.

www.modelrailroadcontrolsystems.com). The EBF31A battery-feed circuit board keeps operating current to 62 milliamps so the carbon particles are protected. Plus, the telephone network itself is important to limiting the current.

Let's take a look at building a simple telephone system using vintage handsets along with parts from MRCS.

Series vs. modern circuits

For comparison let's take a look at a simple series-wired circuit. The circuit comprises two parallel wires, originating at the power supply and connected along its length by the telephone handsets. The power supply can be a battery or a filtered transformer.

The handsets themselves have to be modified so that the current flows through the receivers and transmitters in series, completing the circuit for each. This creates several problems. First, the handsets are all always powered and therefore on, picking up any noise in the room. The current flow through the receiver can, over time, damage the carbon particle element leading to failure. Variations in the electrical characteristics of the different handsets, particularly receiver and transmitter element resistance, can lead to variations in volume.

Now let's look at the more-modern circuit, **2**. Instead of using a battery or transformer-based DC power supply, it uses something called an EBF31A battery feed circuit board, **3**. This circuit, designed by Seth and his partners, is based on old telephone-company designs but slimmed down and with additions to meet the needs of model railroaders. In addition to a connector for a 24V switching power supply, it provides a standard modular telephone jack to connect to a telephone network, a 3.5mm connector for a loudspeaker, and screw terminals for hard-wiring the telephone and power connections. With this circuit board and a telephone network extension adapter you can set up a phone system in a few minutes using unmodified telephones as long as they are fully operational.

The tip and ring connections on the EBF31A are protected against shorting. There is a blocking diode on the power input for protection, and since the telephones are not polarity sensitive there is no potential problem there. That said, you should not install these outside or run a connection to another building without specialized

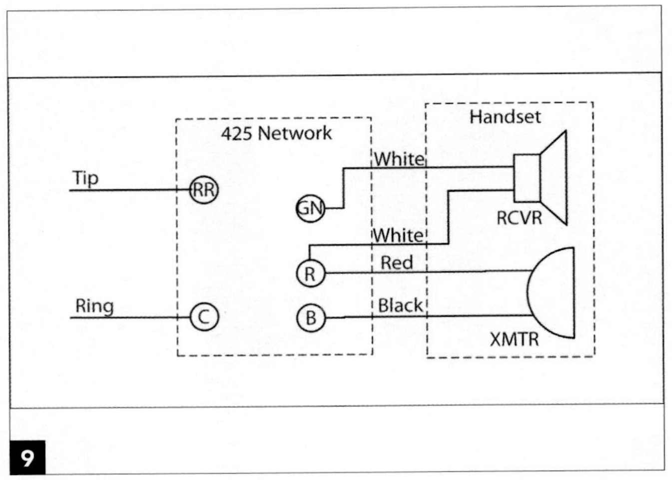

9 This diagram shows where to connect the wires to the female quick-connects on the speech network board. *Courtesy Seth Neumann, MRCS*

10 Follow the wiring diagram in 9 to attach wires from the main network cable to the "RR" and "C" contacts using the screw terminals.

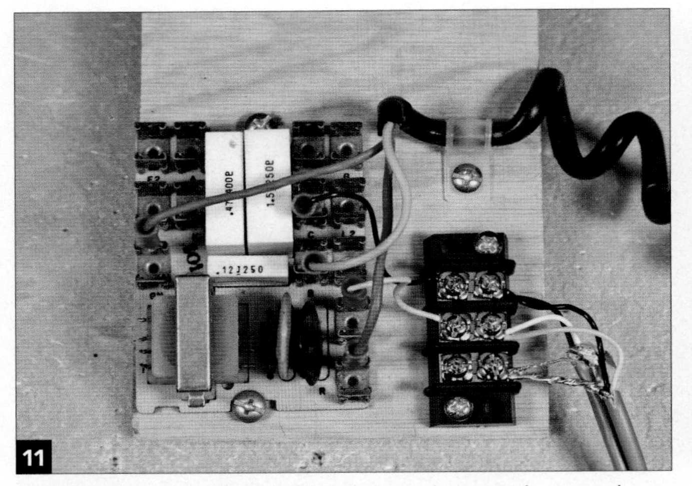

11 Connect the wires from the handset to the speech network "B", GN", and "R" contacts on the speech network board.

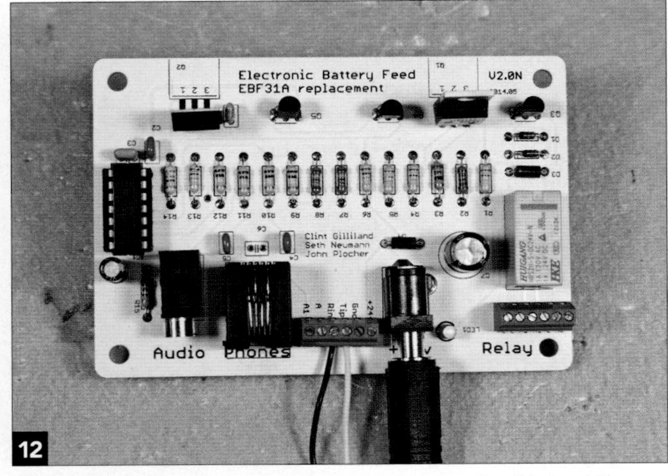

12 Screw terminals are provided on the battery feed board for the tip and ring wires. The red LED is illuminated, indicating a phone on the line is off the hook.

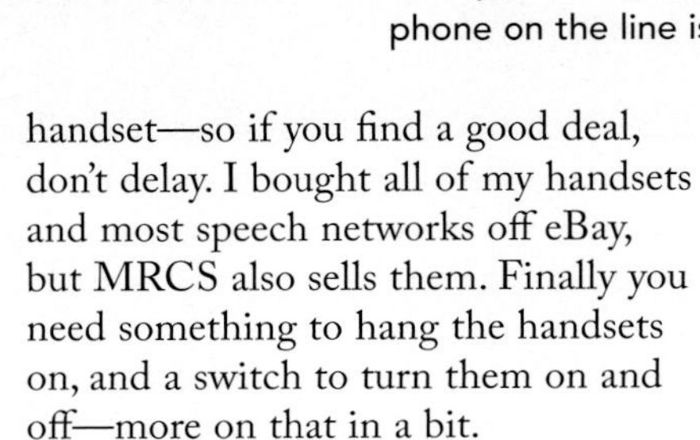

gas tube protectors to prevent the system from acting as a ground path for lightning.

Although using complete working telephones and the MRCS battery feed circuit board is likely to be faster, it also may be the more-expensive option. I wanted to be able to use just the handsets and not have complete telephones hanging or sitting around the layout. This approach has both positives and negatives.

First, because complete vintage telephones are often expensive, you can save money buying just the components you need. The speech network boards, **4**, which would come as part of a complete telephone, have to be purchased separately—one for each handset—so if you find a good deal, don't delay. I bought all of my handsets and most speech networks off eBay, but MRCS also sells them. Finally you need something to hang the handsets on, and a switch to turn them on and off—more on that in a bit.

Wiring

You have a couple of wiring options. Although it only takes two wires for the network, Seth recommends using individual Cat3/5 ethernet cables for two reasons. First, the Cat3/5 cables have four twisted pairs of conductors, which help prevent electronic noise and interference from other layout wiring. Also, the extra wires can be used to add options such as a buzzer or lamp so the dispatcher can "call" a station agent or crew. LEDs can also be wired into the handset hanger or fascia to either warn crews when someone else is talking on the network or to serve as a notice for crews to call in when they reach that station.

Your first decision is whether to install the Cat3/5 cables or to use shielded multiple-conductor cables, which may be cheaper. Cat5 is relatively inexpensive—I found it at a local big box store for $18 per 100-foot roll. Since I already had 200 feet of shielded two-conductor cable I decided to give it a try. To manage all the wires under the layout I used a Gardner Bender low voltage stapler as it is designed specifically for installing

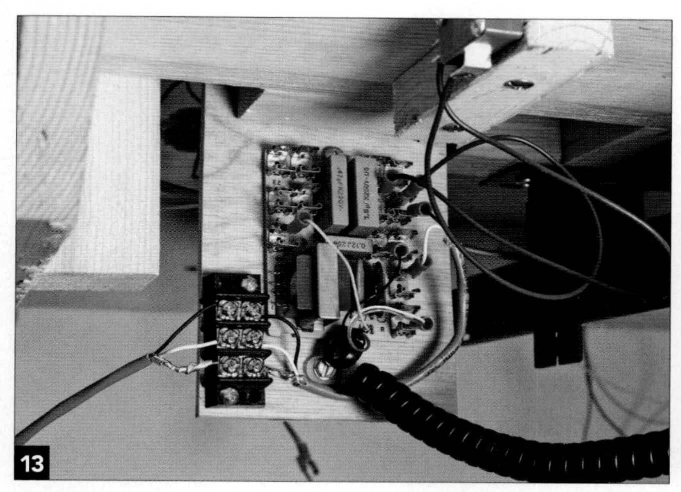

The mounting board makes it easy to attach the completed network station to a joist under the layout.

The handset holder is a 2"-diameter hole in the shelf with a 1½"-wide slot connecting it to the front edge. The switch is mounted at the rear edge of the hole.

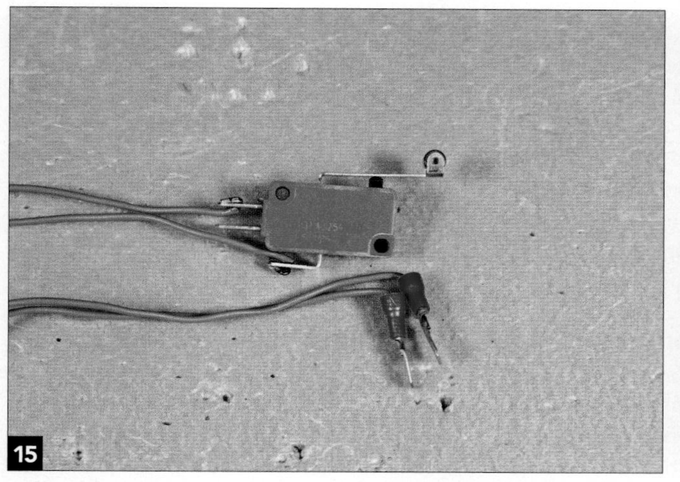

An SPDT snap-switch installed under the handset hole in the shelf serves as the hook switch for each handset.

When the handset is resting in the holder the switch is closed, turning off the telephone circuit to that handset. When it is lifted off the "hook" the circuit is turned on.

Cat3/5 and similar cables. The staples have a raised "loop" along the top that holds the cable without cutting into it.

After stringing the main cable around the layout, I prepared a mounting board for the handset, speech network board, and wiring terminals. I used ¼" plywood, but hardboard would work. I cut the plywood into 3"x6" rectangles; however, you may want to use bigger boards if you plan to add options to the network (more on that in a bit). I attached the speech network circuit board using screws with the heads gripping the edge of the circuit board, **5**. Next I added a three-position screw terminal to the board for attaching the main network cable. I then attached the handset cord, securing it with a ⅛" or ¼" nylon cable clamp depending on the cord thickness, **6**.

I added male quick-connects to the ends of the wires coming from the handsets, **7**. The white and red wires in type G handsets go to the same contact, so I used one male connector for both. If you decide to use older E or F handsets, made of Bakelite, there are only three wires with the red wire as common. I found that the male connects I had were a bit too thick for the females on the speech networks, but a little prying with a small screwdriver tip opened them enough to work, **8**—support the female connectors as you do this to prevent breaking them off the board. I later discovered that smaller $3/16$" male connectors are a better fit than my ¼".

With everything attached to the board, following the diagram in **9**, I attached the wires from the main network cable to the "RR" and "C" contacts, **10**. The wire to "RR" is designated as the tip and the one to "C" is the ring. These terms refer back to the days when phono-type jacks were used, thus the tip being the end of the jack and the ring was the contact ring. Typically these would be green and red wires respectively, but if your cables only have other colors, then adopt them as your standard—mine ended up white and black.

I connected the wires from the handset to the "B", GN", and "R"

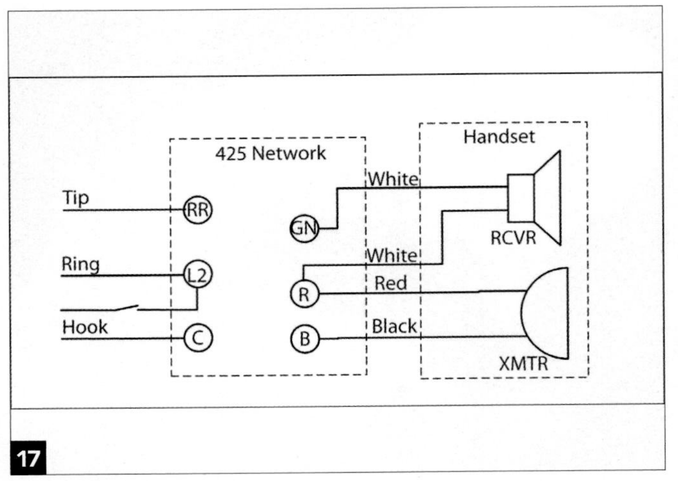

When adding a hook switch, the wires from the switch are connected to the speech network board at contacts "C" and "L2" and the ring wire is moved from "C" to "L2". *Courtesy Seth Neumann, MRCS*

The hook wires (blue) are attached to "C" and "L2" and the ring wire is moved to "L2".

contacts on the speech network board, **11**, following the diagram in **9**. Push these in slowly but firmly and support the female connector to so it doesn't break. Finally, I connected the tip and ring wires to the appropriate screw terminals on the battery feed board, **12**, added a second handset and speech network, plugged in the power supply, and was ready to talk to someone else.

There are a couple of ways to wire all these speech network cards together. If you used Cat3/5 cables, run individual cables back to the dispatcher's desk where the battery feed board is located. Using the individual cables makes troubleshooting easier.

Seth also suggests that if access for pulling all these cables is an issue, then it is possible to daisy-chain the connections with one long bus. Since I was using shielded two-conductor cable, I chose the daisy-chain approach. To address the potential problem with trouble-shooting, I tested each handset and speech network combination as each was completed, and tested each installation as I proceeded out from the dispatcher's desk with the wiring.

If you use shielded cable as I did, ground the drain wire (bare metal wire) in the cable as it may act as a long antenna picking up electronic noise. I connected mine to a cold-water pipe using a grounding clamp (available at hardware stores). Another potential source of noise is the EBF31A circuit board itself. If you detect a hum on the line, run another ground wire to the ground terminal on the center green screw terminal strip on the EBF31A. With everything installed and connected to the network I gave it a test and could clearly hear my wife at the far end of the line.

Phone control and mounting

Now let's add hook switches. "Hook" is an anachronism from when telephone receivers hung on a hook-like switch on a wall or candlestick phone. When the receiver is on the hook the phone is turned off. As soon as the receiver is lifted off the hook the phone is on. Following that, we need a switch connected to each speech network board that will turn it on whenever its handset is off the hook. You can purchase hangers with switches for this, but I made my own built into the 1x6 shelf around the edge of the layout.

I attached the network station mounting board to a joist under the layout, **13**. Then I drilled a 2"-diameter hole in the shelf, centered 1¾" back from the edge, and cut a 1½"-wide slot from the front edge of the shelf back to the hole, **14**. This arrangement allows the handset to be easily dropped into place through the slot so it can sit in the 2" opening.

For the switch I used a single-pole, double-throw (SPDT) snap switch, **15**, wired so that when the switch is off hook the circuit is on. I then mounted the snap switch under the shelf in the hole, **14**, positioned so that when the handset is placed in the opening it rests on the switch spring, closing it and turning off the circuit, **16**.

Adding the hook switch requires a slight modification of the network wiring, **17**. I connected the wires from the switch to the speech network board at contacts "C" and "L2" and moved the ring wire to L2, **18**. Once all the handsets are on hook, the red LED on the battery feed circuit board should go out and only come on when a phone is picked up.

The dispatcher's station is a little different. For it I cut a 6" x 10" plywood rectangle and attached the EBF31A circuit board to the left side using double-sided foam tape. I also added a couple of wood screws but did not seat them (to avoid cracking the board)—the screws are just there just in case the tape fails.

I then attached the speech network board to the right side of the plywood rectangle and a three-position screw terminal in the middle, **19**. I mounted this on the wall behind the dispatcher's desk. Another addition to the dispatcher's station was a foot pedal switch to control the telephone. I ordered the inexpensive one shown in **20** through eBay. It contains a switch similar to that used at the other stations and is wired in the same way.

19

The dispatcher's station board has the EBF31A circuit board, speech network board, and three-position screw terminal strip mounted on a 6" x 10" plywood rectangle. The heavy green wire is the ground, which is connected to a cold-water pipe overhead. Both the network drain wire and the EBF31A ground terminal are connected to the ground wire using one of the screw terminal connections.

20

A foot-pedal switch allows the dispatcher to control the telephone, giving push-to-talk operation and freeing his hands for other chores.

21

A set of speakers connected to the battery feed board allow the dispatcher to listen to conversations without having to hold a receiver.

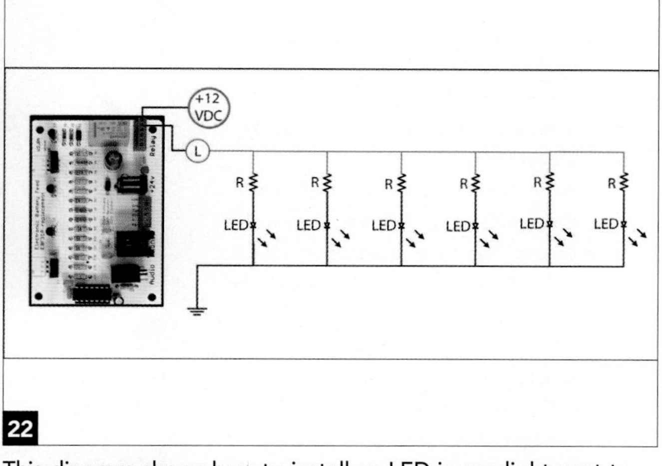

22

This diagram shows how to install an LED in-use light next to each handset. *Courtesy Seth Neumann, MRCS*

Pressing down on the switch with a foot takes the dispatcher's phone off the hook so he's ready to give orders.

I mentioned that the battery-feed circuit board has a connection for a loudspeaker. Luckily I had a pair of stereo speakers left over from an old computer, **21**. I plugged them into the board, turned the switch on, and gave them a test—everything said on the network came out loud and clear. These are perfect for the dispatcher's desk, allowing the dispatcher to hear what is being said without having to hold a telephone receiver.

Since this is a party line network, anyone can pick up a telephone and listen or talk without having to dial or buzz the dispatcher. This can create issues since the battery-feed circuit board can only power about four phones at once. Consequently it is important that your train crews be aware of this so they do not pick up phones unnecessarily. This is a good reason to install the in-use indicator LEDs.

This is simple to do following the diagram in **22**. Hook up a 12VDC power supply wire to the relay contact as shown, then a long wire to the first LED. Continue daisy-chaining the connections around your layout, installing LEDs at each phone station. Connect each 1000-ohm resistor and LED as shown in Chapter 1 and terminate each to the negative wire from the 12VDC power supply. With this wiring, each time a phone is picked up the LEDs all light up, warning train crews that the line is in use.

Thanks to Seth Neumann for his advice on this chapter and for his permission to use several of his diagrams.

A word about vintage telephones

The system described in this chapter should work with just about any telephone used in the last century. Your best chances of getting an unmodified telephone that functions properly will be with those produced since World War II. Be aware that many old telephones found at flea markets, antique stores, and on the Internet have been scavenged for parts or tinkered with over the years. Many have missing parts and disconnected wires. This is especially true of candlestick phones, which are often sold without their original control boxes.

That said, I have an old Kellogg candlestick (top right) without its control box that works well with my system and I didn't have to do a thing to it—I just wired it in like a handset. I also have a railroad dispatchers' phone on a scissors mount that came without a transmitter element and needed rewiring, so be careful what you order online. Restored antique telephones are readily available but at a cost comparable to a new steam locomotive with sound decoder.

Most of the handsets that I used are type G (middle right) and are made of hard plastic that is comfortable to hold. In addition, the receivers and transmitters in them are more efficient and less likely to need replacing. Older type E and F handsets (bottom right) dating back to before WWII are made of Bakelite. They're brittle, heavy, and uncomfortable to hold due to the sharp ridge on the back. They also tend to shatter if dropped on a concrete floor.

Several sources for restored telephones and replacement parts are listed below. Be careful: Telephone collecting and restoration can become almost as obsessive a hobby as model railroading.

Telephone websites:
Model Railroad Control Systems: www.modelrailroadcontrolsystems.com
Old Phone Shop: www.oldphoneshop.com
Old Phone Works: www.oldphoneworks.com
Phoneco: www.phonecoinc.com
Telephone Components: www.telephonecomponents.com

Antique candlestick telephones were a common fixture of dispatcher and depot desks. They add to the atmosphere of layout room or dispatcher's desk.

Relatively modern G-style handsets, which began to appear after WWII, are lightweight and have efficient transmitters and receivers.

Handsets of the F style were common prior to WWII. They're made of Bakelite, a heavy, brittle resin. Mine work fine with the MRCS network.

1

Using a fast clock during operating sessions can help expand the apparent size of a layout, effectively lengthening the time it takes to travel between towns and stations.

CHAPTER FIFTEEN

Add a fast clock for operations

For many years railroads operated based on published timetables, with written train orders from the dispatcher providing additional guidelines. Called timetable and train-order operation, train crews were required to observe schedules and be aware of other trains they were following or meeting. As long as everyone followed the timetable and rules, no two trains would occupy the same section of track at the same time, preventing collisions.

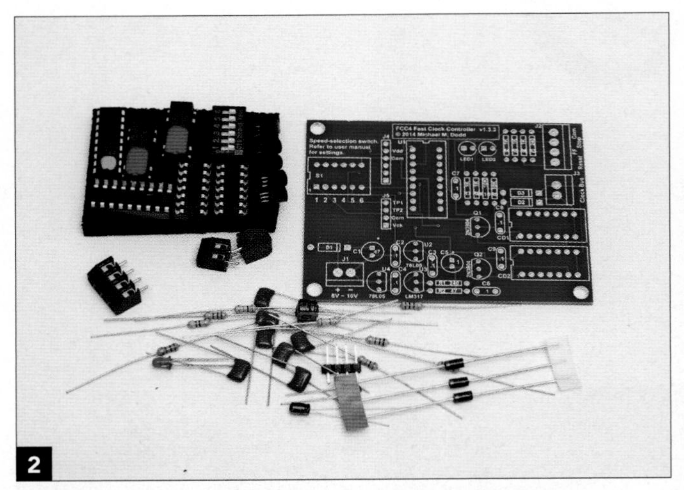
2
Mike Dodd offers a fast clock circuit in kit form or as a completed board. It can control the speed of up to 15 inexpensive clocks placed around your layout room.

3
The mechanisms fit most available dial-type electronic clocks, including those from Heartland Die-Cast which are offered with railroad heralds on the face.

Time, therefore, was (and is) of life-and-death importance to railroads and railroaders. To ensure that everyone was operating on exactly the same schedule, employees were required to carry a pocket watch. To guarantee standardization, railroads specified the watches that could be used. These watches had to be inspected regularly, and employees synchronized them with official "standard clocks" at specified railroad offices. Employees were required to set their watches to company time.

What's a "fast clock"?

It's not practical to provide pocket watches for each participant in a model railroad operating session, but we can certainly provide standard clocks in the layout room for this purpose, **1**.

Model railroaders have long used what is referred to as a fast clock for simulating prototype scheduled operations. The basic idea is to follow a 12- to 24-hour portion of a prototype schedule, but compress it to a two- to four-hour operating session, introducing the concept of compressed or scale time.

The main reason for compressing time is that our model railroads don't scale out to the length of prototype railroads. The length of runs between towns on our layouts is often less than a scale mile, compared to several miles on a prototype. Speeding up the clock means the freight train took 10 minutes in "fast time" to get from town to town, even though the actual time was only a minute or two.

Fast time also allows your operating crews to follow a full day's prototype schedule within a relatively short period of time, without having to wait for an actual hour or two at a siding for an opposing train to arrive.

In the early days of model railroading, before the wonders of modern electronics, a common way for modelers to speed up time was to remove the hour hand from a standard clock and use the minute hand to track the hours. Or they would modify the internal gears to make the clock run faster. With the advent of clocks with electronic mechanisms came the ability to devise circuits to control clock speed.

In the early 1990s I built a fast clock kit for my club's layout. The kit, developed by Mike Dodd, was based on a circuit he designed and shared in the November 1987 *Model Railroader*. The kit allowed controlling the speed at which an electronic quartz clock operated, and made it easy to start and stop the clock.

Mike has kept at it and still offers an updated kit which can control the speed of up to 15 inexpensive clocks, **2**. His circuit allows you to simultaneously start, stop, and reset up to 15 clocks using fast time ratios ranging from 2:1 to 16:1, including fractional ratios (you can choose among 16 standard and 16 fractional ratios).

Mike sells both kits and prebuilt circuit boards as well as modified and unmodified clock mechanisms. Thus, if you have the ability and interest in building a kit you can do so, but if you feel you don't have the skill (or just don't have the time) you can buy ready-to-run versions. His webpage (fastclock.mdodd.com/index.html) offers kits and circuit boards as well as information on selecting and modifying clocks, and also displays instructions for his kits (which can help you decide if the complexity of the kit is within your range to tackle).

There are other fast-clock options for DCC operators, including the fast clock built into Digitrax command stations, which show the time on throttle displays. LogicRail makes a digital fast clock compatible with Digitrax and NCE DCC systems. However, for this project I wanted to be able to use inexpensive electronic dial clocks that can be installed at multiple locations.

Circuit board

Mike's clock mechanisms fit most available dial-type electronic clocks, including those from Heartland Die-Cast which are offered with railroad specific logos on the dial, making them a nice addition to a layout, **3**. You can also purchase Regulator-type wall clocks (the old-fashioned pendulum style) with electronic mechanisms for an antique look. Another option is to

Time is critical to railroad operations. Railroads maintained official standard clocks at various locations, and all other watches and clocks were required to match the standard clocks. *George W. Wickersham II*

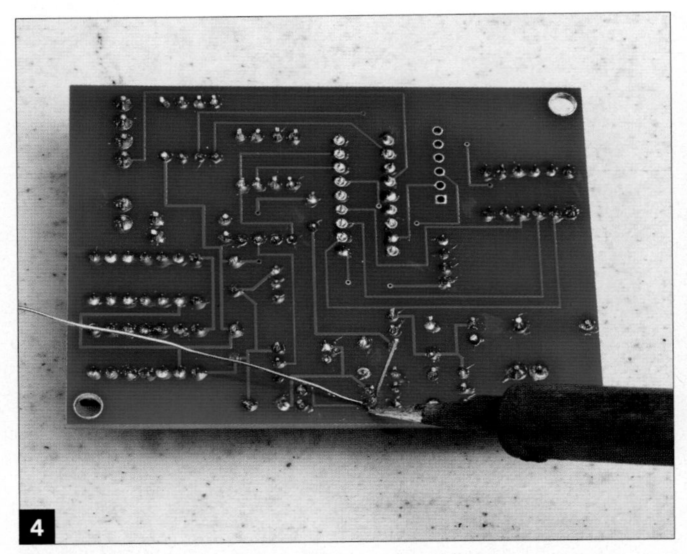

4 The component layout is well-spaced making it easy to get a neat solder job. Use fine rosin-core solder and a fine-tip iron.

5 Fine side cutters or rail nippers work well for trimming each lead just above the solder.

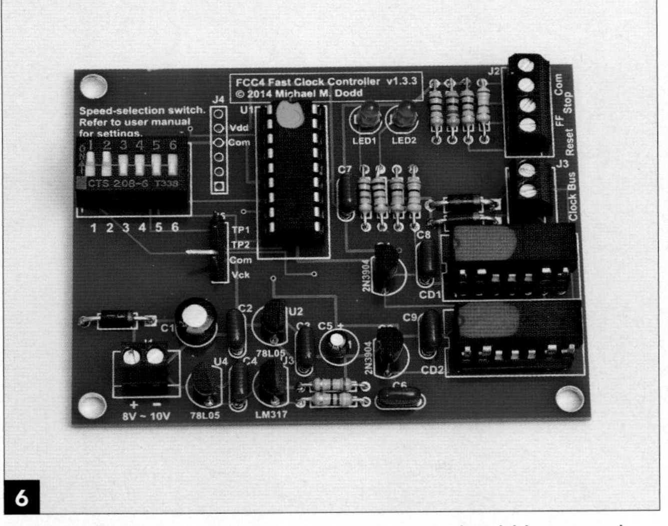

6 The completed circuit board is compact. It should be tested following the instructions.

7 Once you have the mechanism case apart, pull out the metal clips that form the battery contacts.

design your own clock face with logo or herald, print it out, and install it on a commercial clock.

Although this may appear to be a complex project, in reality with the proper tools and Mike's excellent instructions the kit is an easy build. I began by sorting out the various electronic components using Mike's instructions as a guide. It's important to follow the instructions' order of component insertion, as this will allow the smaller components to lay flat while soldering them.

I bent the leads to the .4" spacing required to match the hole spacing of the circuit board, then began the process of inserting and soldering the leads for each component, taking time to cool each one. I used Kester .020"-diameter rosin core solder (do *not* use acid-core solder or additional flux). The fine solder makes it easy to get in close to the board and component leads, **4**, and minimizes the risk of excess solder on the board. I used my Weller WC-100 adjustable soldering station set on medium, but any small 20- to 30-watt iron with a fine tip should do the job.

After soldering each component I used a pair of fine rail nippers to clip each lead off just above the solder, **5**. Once you've completed all the solder joints, scrub the bottom of the board with an old, stiff toothbrush to remove any stray splatters of solder and dislodge any solder bridges. Solder bridges are created when stray bits of solder accidentally connect adjacent component leads. They can cause short circuits and damage components, so look over the board with a magnifier to ensure the board is clean.

Once the board is completed, **6**, go through the check-out and test procedures outlined in the instructions. I know it's tempting to just hook up a modified clock mechanism, turn on the power, and see if it works. However, you don't want to let the magic smoke

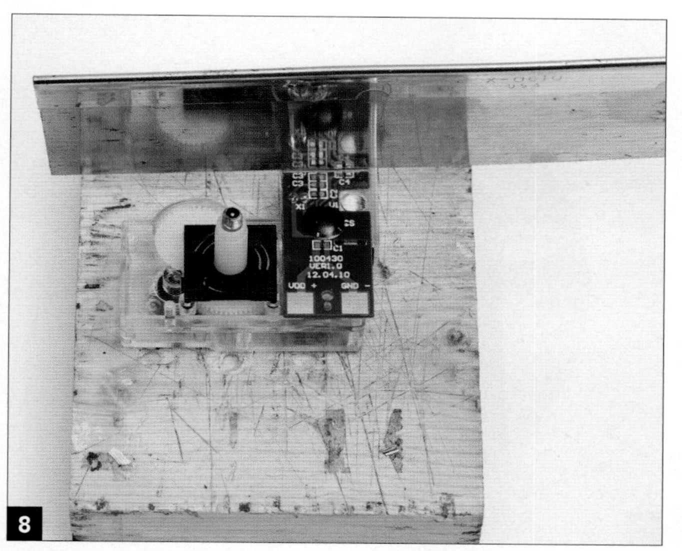

8

A razor saw works well for trimming the circuit board in front of the two solder bumps.

9

I snapped the circuit board while pressing down on the solder bumps to keep that section of the board from breaking loose.

10

I soldered the 1K ohm resistor to the solder bump on the right side of the remaining circuit board and installed it on the mechanism.

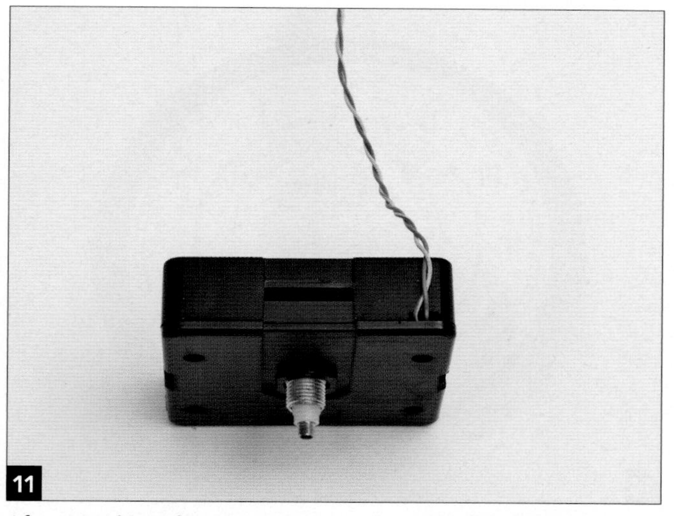

11

After attaching the wires, a ¼" notch in the case allows the wires to exit.

out of any components, so take a few minutes and follow the instructions.

Clock

A modified clock is necessary for the tests, so here's how I prepared one of my Southern Railway clocks. First, use a small screwdriver blade to open the two clips located on the sides of the mechanism, being careful not to break them. A knife blade inserted between the two halves of the case helped pop them apart as I pried on the clip. Once you have the case apart, **7**, pull out the metal clips that form the battery contacts—these can be discarded.

The directions offer two different methods for modifying the circuit board. I recommend the second method since the first—unsoldering using a wick—is difficult at best.

I pulled out the electronics and gearbox and removed the small Phillips-head screw from the circuit board. Using a razor saw I cut through the circuit board in front of the two solder bumps, **8**. Go slowly and inspect your work frequently: You don't want the blade to suddenly cut all the way through the board and damage the transparent case. I cut almost all the way through, then snapped the circuit board while pressing down on the solder bumps to prevent that section of the board from breaking loose, **9**.

After cutting each lead on a 1K ohm resistor to about ⅛" and bending one to a 90 degree angle, I soldered the straight end to the solder bump on the right side of the remaining circuit board, **10**. Then I stripped about ⅛" of insulation from the provided wires, soldered one to the solder bump on the left and the other to the end of the bent resistor lead. I then cut a ¼" access notch in the case where the wires would exit and reassembled the mechanism, **11**.

The mechanism was ready to go into the clock. I flipped the clock on its face, removed the six screws holding

Removing the clock hands was easy with a pair of angled tweezers. Work carefully to not damage the hands or face.

The old mechanism was held in place by clips on the back, which made it easy to remove.

Once the mechanism dropped into place I flipped it on its back to install the new hands.

The minute hand sits loosely on the shaft and is held in place by the small gold acorn nut, giving it a finished look.

the backplate in place, and removed it. The existing clock hands were held in place by friction, so it was easy to gently pry them off until using a pair of angled tweezers, **12**. The mechanism itself was held in place by a couple of clips on the back, which made it easy to remove, **13**.

With the old mechanism removed I snipped off a pair of cast-on plastic nubs where the new mechanism would sit and popped it into place. Unfortunately the clips didn't perfectly match so I removed a thin layer of plastic from the case where they engaged by scraping it with the edge of a hobby knife blade.

With the mechanism dropped into place I flipped it on its back to install the new hands, **14**, first installing the large gold washer and nut while being careful not to damage the faceplate. The hour hand was a press fit onto the shaft. Bend the hand slightly upward if needed to keep it from dragging on the faceplate. The minute hand sits loosely on the shaft and is held in place by the small gold acorn nut, giving it a finished look, **15**. To complete the job I set the hour and minute hands to 12 o' clock, replaced the backplate, and reinstalled the screws.

I connected the two wires from the clock to the screw connectors on the board at J3—orientation doesn't matter. I then connected a couple of wires to the COM connector on J2 and the wires from the regulated 9VDC power supply to J1, being careful to get the polarity correct, then went through the tests.

The final process was to add the control switches and install them and the circuit board in an enclosure or control panel. For switches, single-pole/single-throw (SPST) on/off toggles are ideal for all but the reset, for which is recommended a momentary-contact pushbutton. Since I had about 100 SPDT switches left over from an old control panel I decided to use

16 I used a combination of toggle and pushbutton switches to control the fast clock.

17 The graphics were done on a computer. After printing and laminating the overlay, I punched holes in it and attached it to a black plastic project box, then installed the switches.

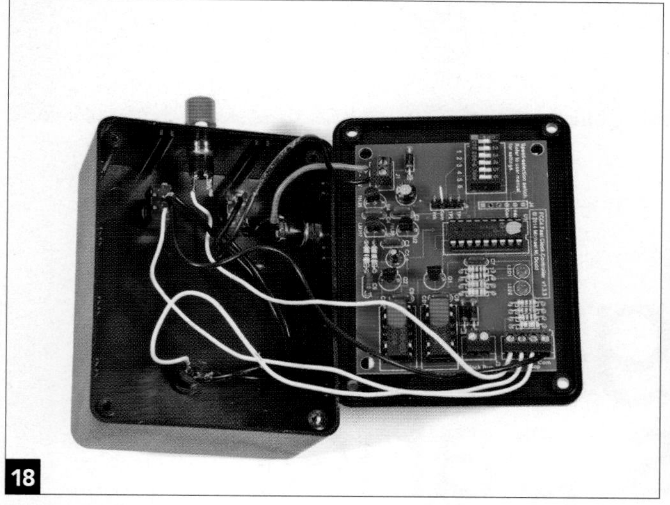

18 I installed the circuit board in the top of the box using double-sided foam tape.

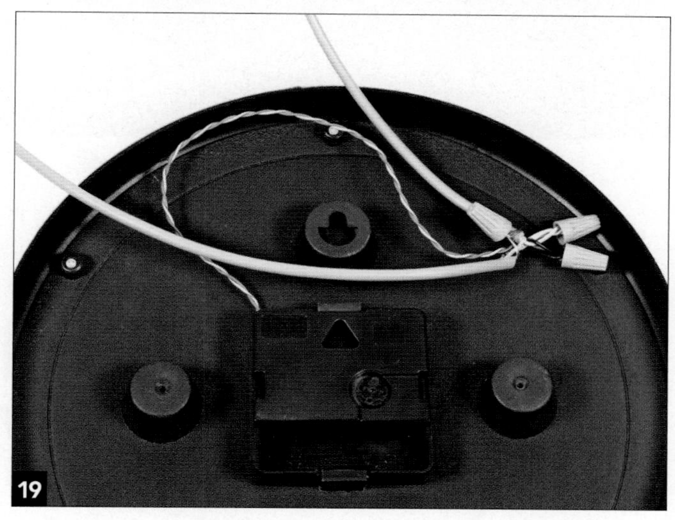

19 I ran a two-wire cable from the controller to the first clock, connected the wires, and then daisy-chained it to the next one and so on. The bare wire is the shield drain.

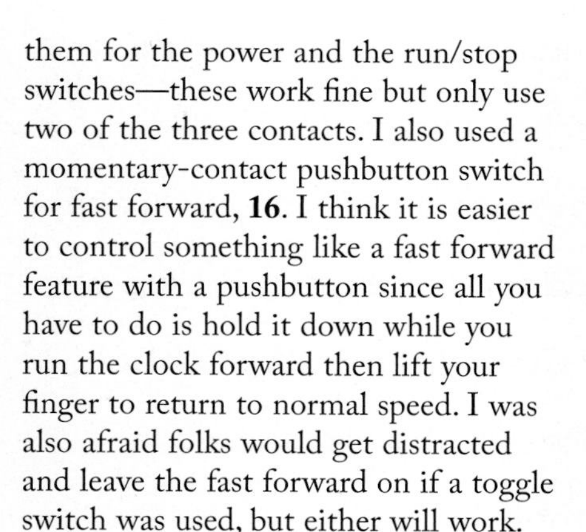

them for the power and the run/stop switches—these work fine but only use two of the three contacts. I also used a momentary-contact pushbutton switch for fast forward, **16**. I think it is easier to control something like a fast forward feature with a pushbutton since all you have to do is hold it down while you run the clock forward then lift your finger to return to normal speed. I was also afraid folks would get distracted and leave the fast forward on if a toggle switch was used, but either will work.

Using a computer graphics program, I made up a control panel overlay following the example in the instructions and had it laminated at an office-supply store. I punched holes in the overlay and attached it to a black plastic project box I got from All Electronics, **17**, using double-sided Scotch tape. After drilling mounting holes for the toggle and pushbutton switches, I installed the circuit board in the top of the box using double-sided foam tape, **18**.

Installing and wiring the clocks is pretty straightforward. I ran a two-wire cable from the controller to the first clock, connected the wires, and then daisy-chained it to the next one and so on, **19**. Keep the cable away from any AC and DCC cables to prevent interference. It's also is a good idea to use shielded cable. You can connect as many as 15 clocks to a bus up to 180 feet long. If you have clocks at opposite ends of a room you can run a bus out in each direction from a centrally placed control panel.

This is one of the easiest circuit kits I have built, and it can help transform the appearance of a layout room or dispatcher's desk and provide a fresh view of operations on your layout.

For more information on operations based on timetables and train orders (and ideas for applying them to a layout), see Tony Koester's book *Realistic Model Railroad Operation, Second Edition* (Kalmbach, 2014).

1

CHAPTER SIXTEEN

Build a magnetic dispatcher's panel

Computer graphics allow building almost any style of dispatcher's panel, from modern to classic. Magnetic indicator tabs can be combined with occupancy lights or control switches as needed.

In model railroad operating sessions the role of the dispatcher varies greatly depending on how realistic the owner wants it to be. A basic schematic panel, **1**, will help the dispatcher control train movements, and you can make the panel as complex as needed for your layout. Prototype versions ranged from complex Centralized Traffic Control panels, **2**, **3**, to basic schematics used by dispatchers in timetable and train-order territory, **4**.

The dispatcher is responsible for routing trains while keeping them safely separated. This Centralized Traffic Control (CTC) panel gives dispatchers full control over signals and turnouts at passing sidings along a line. *Donald Sims*

This Union Switch & Signal CTC board has a schematic track diagram that includes lights that indicate the presence of trains. The bottom row of numbered levers controls signals; the row above controls turnouts. *Harold A. Edmonson*

Many dispatching panels were much simpler—just a diagram, with possibly occupation indicator lights. Dispatcher Edward Brunner is working the Rock Island's eastern Iowa lines at the railroad's Des Moines office in the 1970s. *R.B. Olson*

On prototype railroads that used timetable and train orders (TT&TO), the dispatcher typically sat at a desk with a time sheet and other paperwork to keep track of train locations, **4**. Train crews aligned turnouts at passing sidings based on train schedules and orders transmitted by the dispatcher. The dispatcher would communicate with train crews primarily through orders telegraphed or telephoned to a station agent who in turn handed them up to crews in passing trains.

With the introduction of Centralized Traffic Control (CTC) came complex control panels like those in **2** and **3**. These allowed the dispatcher to follow train movements on a section of railroad and gave him the power to align turnouts and set signals for the desired route. This greatly reduced the number of train orders needed and minimized the amount of communication needed with agents and train crews.

A full-blown CTC panel is an expensive option for a model railroad, although you can have one custom built. Although beyond the scope of this book, computerized versions with digital simulations of CTC boards are possible with the Java Model Railroad Interface (JMRI) PanelPro program (see jmri.org for details and examples).

Many model railroaders have found that CTC panels and related signaling, although fun and dramatic, provide plenty of operating interest for the dispatcher but not enough for train crews. Opting for a simple dispatcher's panel and train sheet and using TT&TO operations instead of CTC keeps the dispatcher and crew members alike far more involved in operational decisions.

The dispatcher's panel I designed for my HO Piedmont Southern layout has custom graphics for the schematic, mounted on a thin steel sheet. This allows magnetic markers to be used to indicate train locations. It provides the feel of a dispatcher's office without the expense and time of building a full CTC system.

Creating graphics

We'll start with a large sheet of paper, a ruler, some pencils, and erasers. You need to draw a straight line diagram of your model railroad, **5**. This doesn't need to be pretty, and after a bunch of editing it may look quite messy, but that's OK—just get something down on paper. You don't need to include every industry spur, yard track, siding, and other details. The goal is to provide your dispatcher with the important features on the main line. Include interchange tracks, crossings, passing sidings, and stations or other points where a train might have to stop on the main line. Show "choke points" like gantlet tracks or single-track areas on double-track lines. I also include things like the helix located at the midpoint of my layout, and—on double-track section—the locations of crossovers.

With your diagram completed it's time for step two, re-creating it in a computer graphics program. Adobe Illustrator and Photoshop are great, but Microsoft Word or any program capable of drawing lines and text will do the job.

First put down a nice background such as the green and black pattern used on the Union Switch and Signal

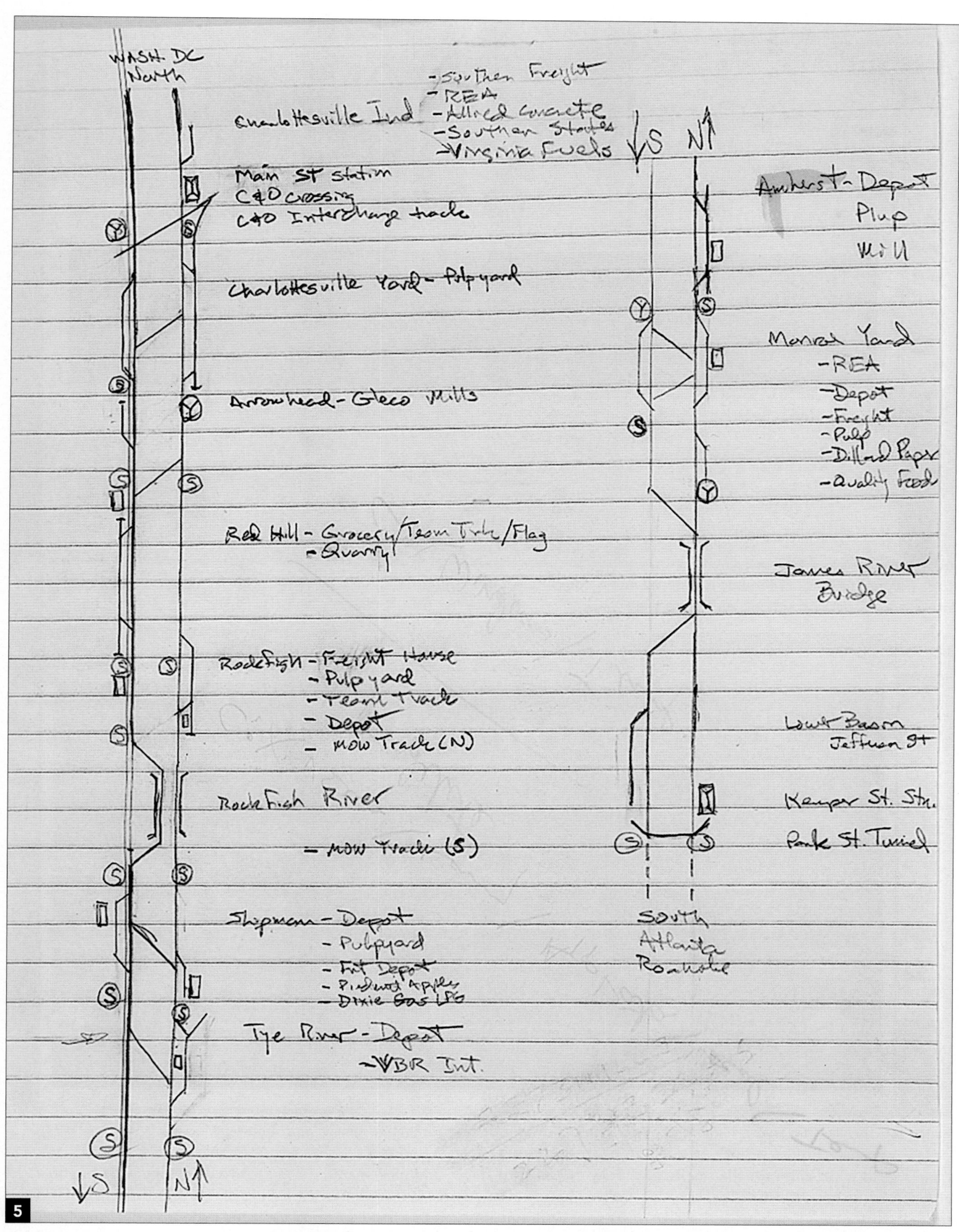

5

The track plan should be converted to a straight line drawing on paper. This one has a lot of information not included on the final diagram, but as I said it can get messy.

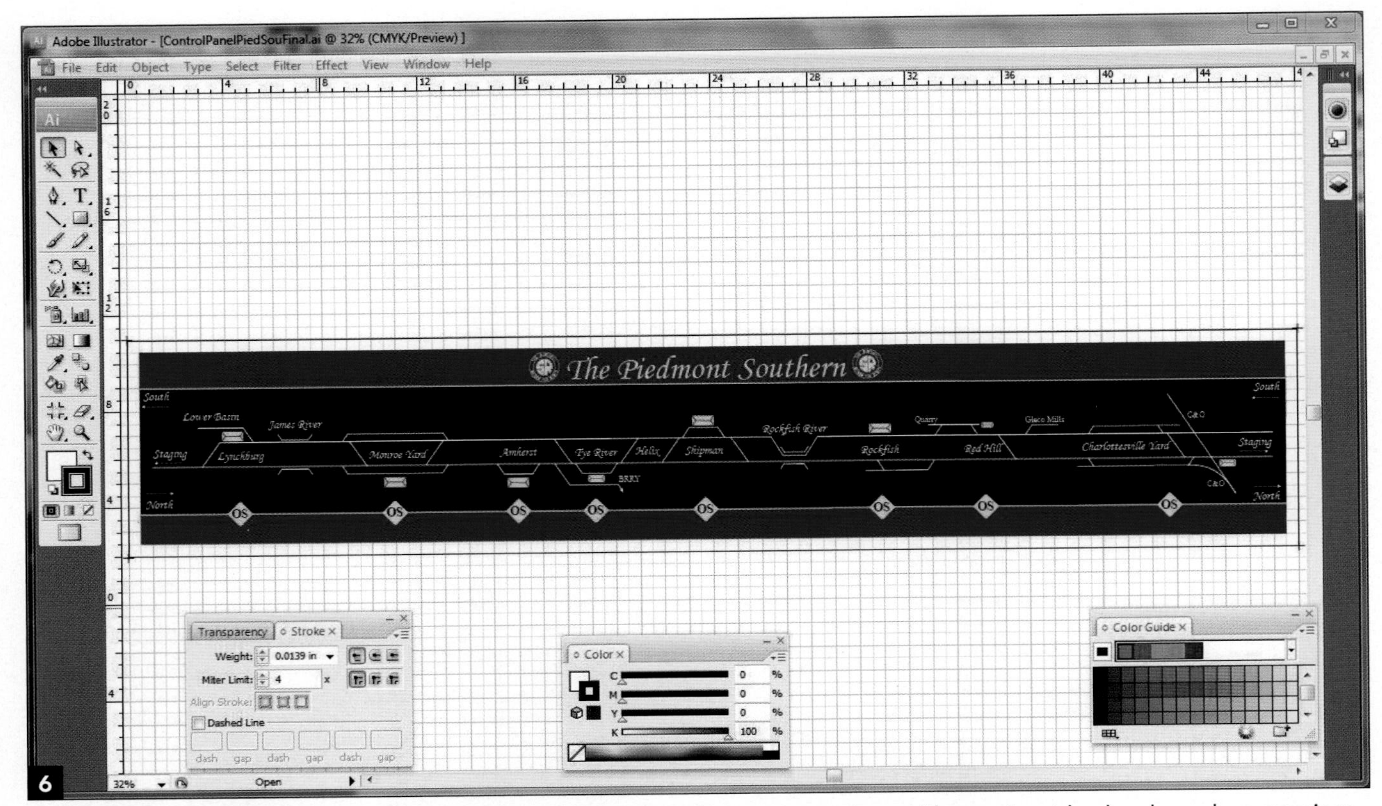

The straight-line track schematic is entered into a computer graphics program along with prominent landmarks such as crossings, interchanges, passing sidings, and crossovers.

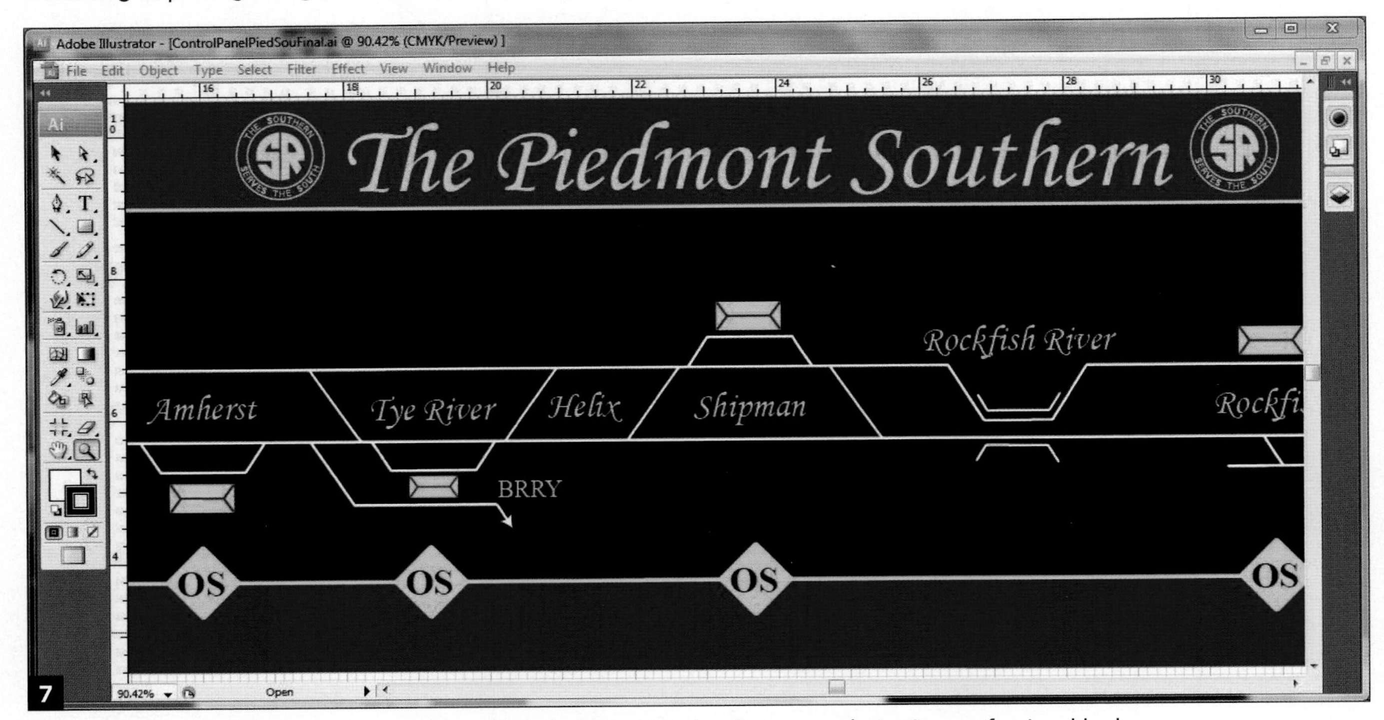

Fancy touches like the layout name and heralds help customize the diagram and give it a professional look.

panels. Add white lines for the tracks and special features like bridges, tunnels, sidings, and crossovers. I used large yellow text so it would stand out, **6**. Don't forget details like arrows to show direction of travel, and placement of staging yards, junctions, and stations. At your option you can get as fancy as you desire with your layout name and heralds, **7**.

Once you're happy with the final artwork, save it as a PDF or JPG file, place it on a thumb drive, and head for the local print shop or office supply store—I ended up at a local Staples.

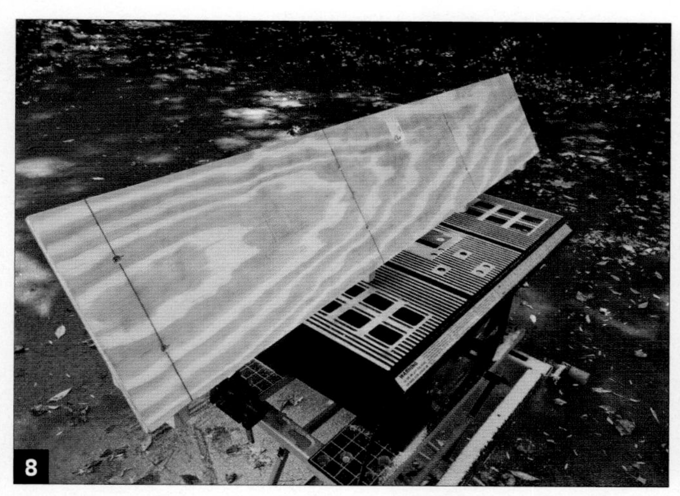

Cut a piece of ½" or thicker plywood the size of the graphic. It will serve as the backer board for the sheet steel.

Wooden trapezoids cut from 1 x 6 lumber are used to support the panel at a slight angle.

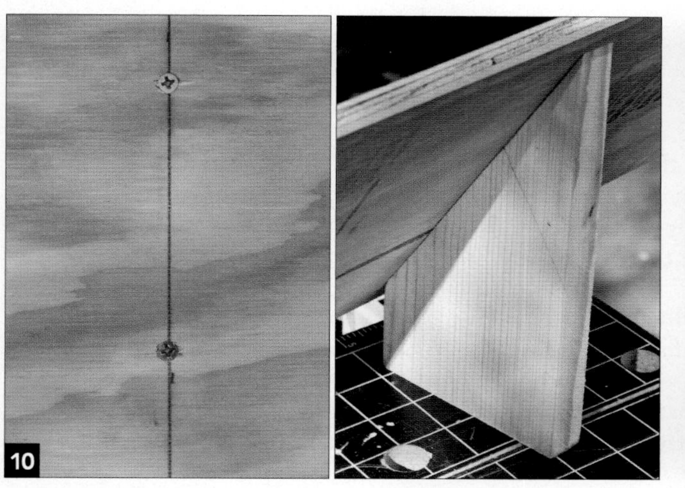

Attach the wooden supports to the plywood backer board using glue and wood screws. Make sure the supports are aligned properly and square to the backing board.

Have a metal shop cut a rectangle of thin sheet steel to the same dimensions as the vinyl diagram. This will serve as the magnetic surface, so make sure the material is steel and not aluminum or other non-magnetic metal.

Custom print or graphic display businesses are another possibility, and many offer additional special design and printing options.

The store I went to offered several possible options including printed paper posters, laminated prints, and vinyl banners. I chose a vinyl banner for durability. Vinyl is available in various thicknesses, measured in ounces (4- to 15-ounce is common). Because I was going to be attaching the diagram to solid backing, I opted for the thinner 4-ounce version (thicker material may interfere with the ability of magnets to stick to the panel). I was a bit concerned about the durability, since dispatchers would be continually moving and sliding magnets across the surface, but I was assured it would hold up—and it has.

The final version of my diagram measured 9" x 48", so I was a bit worried about the price—but it came in at under $10, which I consider a bargain. Due to a misprint I ended up with an extra diagram, so as a test I applied a coat of Minwax spray polyurethane varnish to increase the durability. The satin finish works well, helps keep glare down, and provides a protective overcoat.

Building the panel

I carefully measured the vinyl print to make sure the sheet metal and plywood backers would be cut to the correct dimensions. This isn't all that critical since if the diagram is too big it can be trimmed once it is glued down, and if it comes up a bit short on one side or the other we can do some final adjusting when getting the metal and plywood sheets. Gaps can also be hidden using corner molding.

Start by cutting a piece of plywood to match the size of your graphic. If you don't have a table saw or circular saw, most lumberyards and big-box home improvement stores will cut a piece of plywood for you for a nominal fee (and save you the hassle and the stray sawdust), **8**. I used ½" plywood; thicker will work fine but be quite heavy, and thinner plywood will start to feel flimsy.

The supports are cut from 1x6 pine. The final dimensions will depend on

12

A coat of construction adhesive, such as Liquid Nails, allows you to apply the sheet metal and adjust it before the glue sets.

13

Use a putty knife to spread the adhesive into a thin layer. Make sure you cover the surface completely.

the size of your diagram and the angle at which you mount it. A table saw or miter saw will provide accurate, square cuts (you can also have the lumberyard do it for you).

Cutting the 1x6 diagonally produces two right angle trapezoids. I used a 55 degree angle and then narrowed the width a bit to fit completely on the back of the plywood. These are attached to the back of the plywood and serve as supports, **9**. I used four supports for my 48"-long panel.

Attach the 1x6 supports to the rear of the plywood backer board. I used wood glue and wood screws in countersunk holes to secure the supports, **10**. Make sure the screwheads are slightly recessed so they don't interfere with installing the metal plate in the next step.

If there's any flex in the plywood I suggest adding 1x1 strips to the back at the top and bottom. These will also serve as mounting blocks if you decide to add a frame or trim.

Head to a local sheet-metal shop and have them cut a sheet of thin sheet steel sized to match your diagram, **11**. Also ask them to smooth the edges to prevent cuts. This piece need not be thick since it will be installed atop plywood—it just needs to be steel, so bring a magnet with you to make sure.

Apply a coat of construction adhesive (I used Liquid Nails), **12**, to the plywood backing board and spread it evenly with a plaster or putty knife, **13**. This adhesive sets up slowly, allowing time to adjust the position of the metal sheet. Press the metal sheet in place, and when it's in proper position, lay the metal/plywood sandwich face down on a flat surface and add some weights. Allow a couple of days for it to dry thoroughly.

Applying the diagram

This step is critical for the panel's appearance. First, use alcohol or another vinyl-compatible solvent to clean the metal surface of any oil or other contaminants. Once this is dry, lay the diagram on the board to make sure the vinyl fits perfectly. If the vinyl overhangs the edge, apply it first before trimming it.

I did a couple of practice runs before spraying on the adhesive, and found it easiest to control by rolling the vinyl onto the sheet metal beginning at one end. Spray an even coat of 3M Super 77 adhesive on the sheet metal and roll the diagram onto the adhesive-coated surface, **14**. Using a soft towel, smooth the surface to work out any air pockets. When that's done, place the diagram facedown, add some weights to it, and let it dry 24 hours.

You can leave the edges bare or frame them with plain or decorative molding as I did. After measuring and cutting four pieces of molding, I glued and nailed them to the edges of the plywood backer board, **15**. The finished magnetic panel, **1**, gives the dispatcher's desk a professional look.

Markers and operations

You can make your own magnetic markers using flexible magnetic strip material from Amazon, Home Depot, craft stores, and other sources. I recommend flat sheets as opposed to rolled material, which sometimes doesn't lay flat.

Micro-Mark (www.micromark.com) also sells a kit that includes a 6" x 24" metal panel, adhesive line tape, self-stick letters and numerals, magnetic strip material, and "train"-shaped plastic overlays. The individual components of the kit are sold separately so you can purchase additional metal panels for a bigger board, or the magnets and overlays for the magnetic train markers.

I used the Micro-Mark magnets and vinyl overlays. The Micro-Mark magnets are ½" wide and about 1" long and come with an adhesive backing—the vinyl overlays are cut to fit on them, **16**. I used a Brother label maker to create adhesive overlays with the train numbers.

It can be difficult to pick the magnets off the panel, so I made handles by cutting the pin portion from colored pushpins and gluing them to the markers. You can use different colors of pins for different train types. For example, mine are red for first class trains, green for second class, blue for third class, and yellow for extras.

So how are these panels used during an operating session? The dispatcher simply moves the magnetic markers

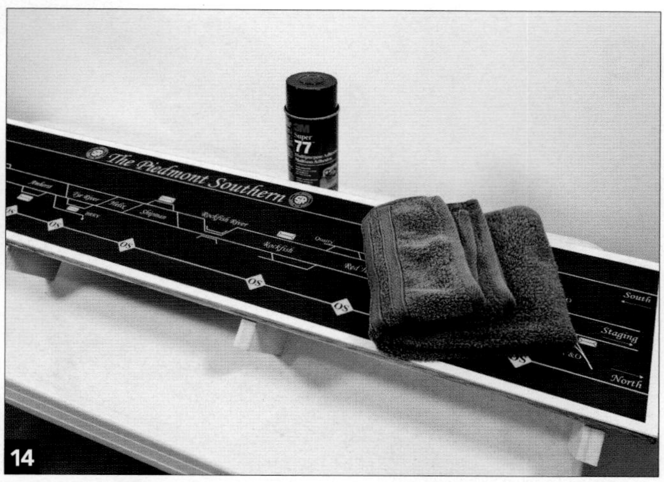

Spray 3M Super 77 adhesive on the sheet metal, making sure to cover it completly. Carefully lay the vinyl print in place, then smooth it with a folded towel to get rid of trapped air pockets.

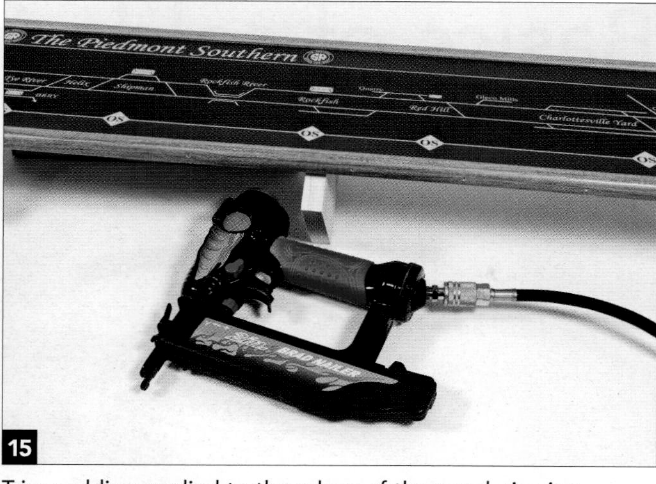

Trim molding applied to the edges of the panel give it a finished look and protect the sides. I used an air-powered brad nailer, but a hammer and thin finishing nails work as well.

Micro-Mark makes these magnets already cut to shape with arrow points to indicate direction. I added train numbers, which allow the dispatcher to keep track of train locations. I used a label maker for the train numbers; you can also use a computer to print on adhesive-backed labels. The pushpin "handles" (with most of the pin itself removed) make it easy to lift the magnets off the board. The pushpins can also be used to color-code the indicators by train class or type.

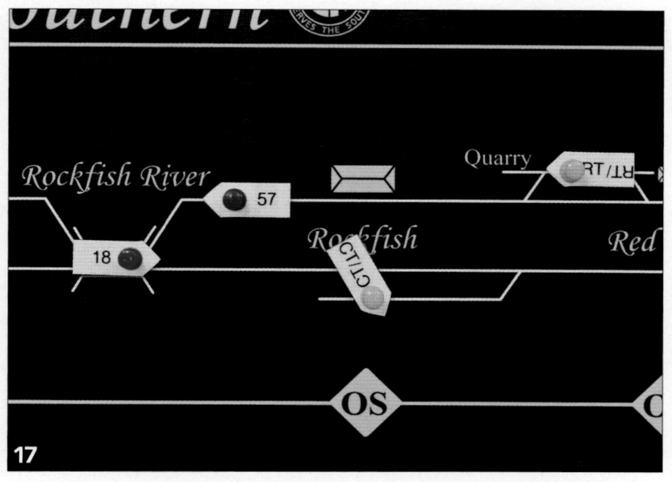

The magnet markers are placed on the diagram on the track where a train is occupying the main line or is in a siding or industry lead. Here train No. 18 is on the Rockfish River bridge while No. 57 waits on the southbound main for it to pass. Farther up the line, the Charlottesville Turn (CT) is blocking both the northbound main and the crossover to the Rockfish siding, and the Rock Train (RT) is safely in the clear on Red Hill Quarry siding.

along the track plan as the train crews call in (using the phone system in Chapter 14). If a train is blocking the main, the magnetic marker can be placed across the track. If a train is off the main in an industrial area or in a siding the marker should be placed there to indicate that the main line is clear, **17**. That way the dispatcher knows the location of each train on the layout and at a glance can decide whether to allow another train to proceed. Think of it as a manual version of a CTC panel.

The yellow "OS" diamonds indicate points where a station operator would call to report a train has passed. The OS is short for "on sheet" and was used by a station agent to tell the dispatcher a train had passed his station. He would call the dispatcher and report "train 55 on sheet at 9:57." I included the OS graphics on the diagram so the dispatcher knows where trains should report in. On my layout, train crews are responsible to do this since most model railroads do not have an agent assigned to each station.

Just a starting point

Use this as a starting point for your own ideas. Feel free to add toggle or pushbutton switches to control turnouts and signals or add indicator lights as shown in Chapters 11 and 12. You can make your own panel as simple or complex as you desire based on your needs and the type of operation on your layout.

You'll find many ideas for operation in Tony Koester's book, *Realistic Model Railroad Operation, Second Edition* (Kalmbach, 2014).

Basics of soldering

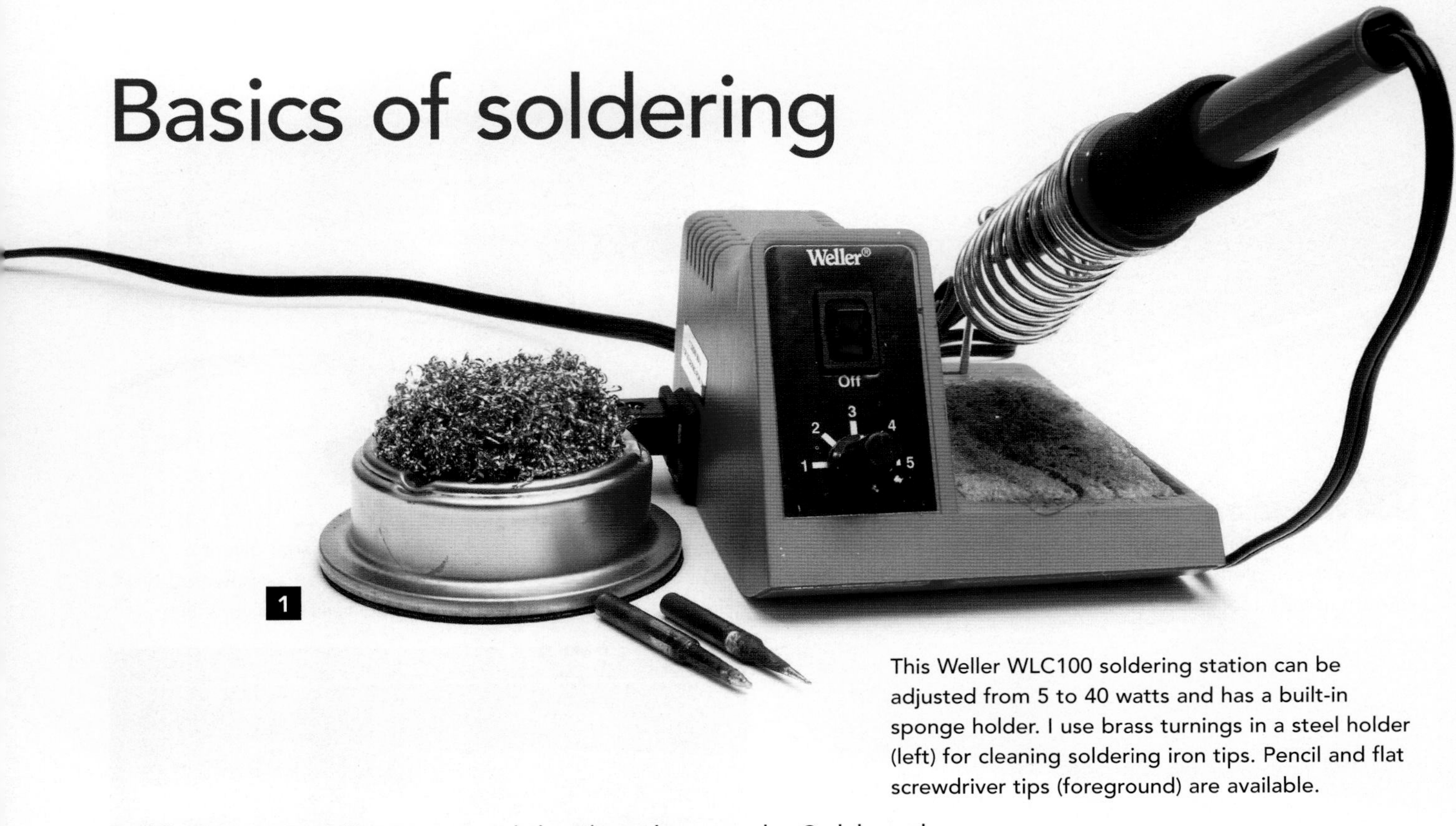

1

This Weller WLC100 soldering station can be adjusted from 5 to 40 watts and has a built-in sponge holder. I use brass turnings in a steel holder (left) for cleaning soldering iron tips. Pencil and flat screwdriver tips (foreground) are available.

Soldering is a skill every model railroader needs. Soldered track feeders, rail joiners, and electrical connections are necessary for reliable Digital Command Control (DCC) operations. Let's take a look at some of the tools that will make your job easier, along with some tips on their use.

The most important tool is a good soldering iron. Fortunately we have a wide array of electronic soldering irons to choose from, but how do you choose? As with most situations, you need to match the tool with the job.

Small electrical components and delicate 28AWG wires call for small, low-wattage irons. However, soldering track feeders and rail joiners works best when you can put a lot of heat on the spot and get out before your ties turn into a pile of molten plastic. So what is your best option?

You can purchase an assortment of irons of different wattages, but I prefer a more flexible approach—a soldering station like my Weller WLC100, **1**. This reliable tool can be adjusted over a range of 5 to 40 watts, giving a maximum temperature of about 900 degrees F.

In addition, Weller designed the handpiece to accept a variety of tips so you can customize it for the job. I typically use a small pencil tip for delicate work and move up to a larger flat screwdriver tip for rail joiners and other projects requiring a lot of heat. The heating element is replaceable and can be purchased separately should you ever burn one out (I've replaced only one in 10 years of heavy use).

Solder varies in composition, with tin and lead in a 60:40 ratio common for model railroading uses. However, 63:37 solder is also popular. An important distinction is that 60:40 solder has different temperatures at which it becomes a liquid and a solid, existing as a paste between these two points, whereas 63:37 solder passes from liquid to solid at 361 degrees. This is important, since if a 60:40 solder joint is moved while cooling, it might not form a solid connection, whereas the 63:37 solder solidifies immediately.

Hard solders containing silver are also available and can have melting points near 900 degrees F. These would be used for making turnouts and detailing brass locomotives. Some people also prefer lead-free solder. Solder is available in varying diameters. I use Kester 60:40 rosin-core solder with a diameter of .022". The small diameter makes it suitable for any job from small electrical components to rail joiners and track feeders.

Flux prevents the formation of metal oxides during heating and allows the solder to make a solid, electrically conductive joint. There are two basic kinds of flux, acidic and non-acidic. Acid fluxes can result in later corrosion, so avoid them for model railroad use.

Instead, use a non-corrosive rosin flux. It's available in both liquid and paste formulations and leaves a non-corrosive residue that can be wiped away with alcohol. I use a rosin paste flux, **2**, from RadioShack. Similar products are available from electrical suppliers and on Amazon.com.

Working with flux is pretty straightforward, but you have to get the heat and solder applied before you burn off all the flux. That's why it's important to use a soldering iron big enough to heat the work quickly and evenly without overheating the flux.

If you burn off the flux, then the metal is likely to oxidize before the solder joint is complete, making the joint weak and prone to failure. This is one reason many people prefer rosin core solder, with the flux making up 1 to 3 percent of the wire. I also apply a small amount of paste solder on large joints as well.

It's important to keep the soldering iron tip clean and tinned. Don't use sandpaper or any other abrasive to clean the iron tip. Soldering iron tips have a copper core covered with iron. If you sand off the iron coating, the tip will be ruined. Weller makes a cleaning bar specifically for cleaning really dirty tips, but if you use the right solder, flux, and regular cleaning, you should never need one.

For years my common cleaning practice was to keep a moist sponge next to the soldering iron and wipe off any excess solder or residue on the sponge between uses. The WLC100 comes with a built-in sponge holder. Keep the sponge moist, not sopping wet, and the tip will come clean with a quick swipe.

More recently, however, I've been using a tip cleaner made of brass turnings in a metal holder. A quick poke of the tip into the brass turnings will remove any excess solder and residues, and you don't have to worry about keeping a sponge moist.

Tinning is the process of applying a small amount of solder to the soldering iron tip. This makes it easier to apply heat quickly to the components being joined. It's a good idea to always tin the tip before turning the soldering iron off. The solder protects the tip from oxidation and will prolong its life.

Weller and a number of other companies sell a tip cleaner/tinning paste comprising mainly flux with solder powder in it. By plunging your hot soldering iron tip into the paste, the tip is cleaned and tinned.

Avoiding damage to surrounding materials is another concern when soldering near plastic ties or anything else that can be burned, melted, or distorted. While it's important to quickly apply a lot of heat to a joint, metal components will also conduct that heat to other areas, which can result in damage.

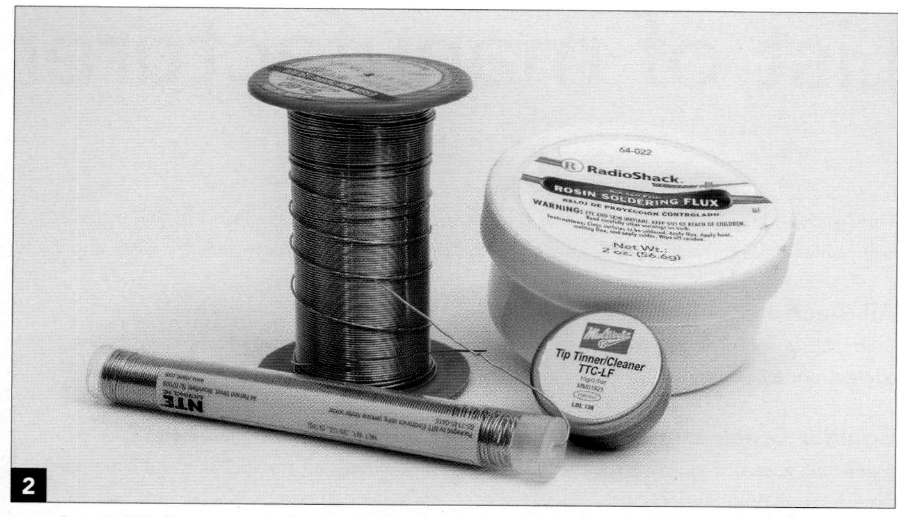

2 I prefer .022" diameter tin/lead 60:40 rosin-core solder. The roll of silver bearing solder in the plastic tube is for special projects. The small container holds a mixture of rosin and solder powder for cleaning and tinning the tip in one step.

3 Heat sinks prevent excess heat from melting ties or damaging sensitive electrical components. Place them between the solder joint and the area you want to protect. Hemostats work well; alligator clips and commercial heat sinks are more compact.

To avoid this problem, use heat sinks to isolate the area to be soldered, **3**. A heat sink can be something as simple as a piece of moist cotton cloth laid over the rails. Excess heat will be consumed by evaporating the water in the cloth, preventing damage elsewhere.

You can also use hemostats clamped on either side of the joint. A couple of small alligator clips or commercial heat sinks will likewise effectively intercept excess heat and are less likely to get in the way while soldering.

For most solder joints, apply a small amount of paste flux with a small brush, then quickly heat the joint with the correct iron tip. Be sure to heat both wires equally. Test the joint by touching the end of a piece of solder wire to it. As soon as the solder melts and starts to flow, apply as much solder as needed, then keep the work perfectly still while the solder cools. If you move the work before the solder solidifies, you may get a weak joint.

One sign of a good joint is a shiny surface appearance. A dull appearance indicates a weak joint, but that can easily be corrected by quickly reheating the solder until it reflows and holding it perfectly still. A quick scrub with alcohol on a stiff brush afterward will remove any rosin flux residue.

List of manufacturers

This list includes websites for most of the companies and products listed in this book. Not all products are still in production, and some companies have gone out of business. To find out-of-production models, try eBay and do a general Internet search.

All Electronics
Bulbs, LEDs, wiring components
allelectronics.com

Boulder Creek Engineering
Electronic accessories and circuits
bouldercreekengineering.com

Circuitron
Switch machines, circuits, and accessories
circuitron.com

City Classics
Structures, interiors, and details
cityclassics.biz

Custom Model Railroads
Turntable kits and accessories
custommodelrailroads.com

DCC Specialties
DCC decoders and accessories
dccspecialties.com

Digitrax
DCC systems and accessories
digitrax.com

Mike Dodd
Fast clock circuits and components
fastclock.mdodd.com/index.html

Jameco Electronics
Motors, lights, and electronic components
jameco.com

Java Model Railroad Interface
Model railroad control software
jmri.com

Kadee
Electromagnetic uncouplers, models
kadee.com

Logic Rail Technologies
Signaling, fast clock, CTC, and other circuits
logicrailtech.com

Micro-Mark
Wiring components and tools
micromark.com

Miller Engineering
Simulated neon signs and lighting
microstru.com

Miniatronics
Bulbs, connectors, and accessories
miniatronics.com

Model Railroad Control Systems
Phone and communication accessories
modelrailroadcontrolsystems.com

New York Railway Supply
Turntable controls and accessories
nyrs.com

NJ International
HO and N scale signals
njinternational.com

North Coast Engineering
DCC systems and accessories
ncedcc.com

Oregon Rail Supply
Signals and accessories
oregonrail.com

Rob Paisley
Lighting and detection circuits
home.cogeco.ca/~rpaisley4/CircuitIndex.html

Quickar Electronics
Lighting and lighting circuits
www.moreleds.com

Radio Shack
Bulbs, LEDs, and electronic components
radioshack.com

Tam Valley Depot
DCC accessories and electronic circuits
tamvalleydepot.com

Tomar Industries
Signals and components
tomarindustries.com

Wm. K. Walthers
Structures, lights, and accessories
walthers.com

Woodland Scenics
Lighting systems, lights, and accessories
woodlandscenics.com

About the author

Dr. Larry Puckett is a contributing editor for *Model Railroader* magazine and since 2015 has served as the magazine's DCC Corner columnist. Prior to that, Larry served as a contributing editor for *Model Railroading* magazine from 1991 until 2006. He has written more than 200 articles in various magazines including *Model Railroader*, *Model Railroading*, and *Railroad Model Craftsman*. His most recent book, *Wiring Your Model Railroad*, was published by Kalmbach in 2015.

Larry's introduction to model trains came with an O gauge set that he received for Christmas 1958, but his introduction to trains goes back even further. Larry's grandfather worked for the Norfolk & Western and an uncle worked for the Chesapeake & Ohio. It shouldn't come as a surprise that his main modeling interests include railroads of the Southeast, particularly the Southern Railway and the N&W, which serve as the focus of his current HO scale Piedmont Southern layout. He says he became a serious modeler in 1980 after purchasing a copy of *Model Railroader* at a local hobby shop.

A history buff, Larry enjoys researching how prototype railroads operated and then applying that knowledge to model railroading. Larry also enjoys the technical side of the hobby, especially the electronics and the emergence of Digital Command Control. "The introduction of DCC has not only radically changed how we wire and build our model railroads, it has changed how we operate them as well," Larry said. "So for me the electronics go hand in hand with prototype operations."

When not in his train room or turning out an article or DCC Corner column on his computer, Larry enjoys landscape photography and fly fishing for native and wild trout in the many mountain streams of western North Carolina. A retired research scientist, Larry worked with the U.S. Geological Survey for 33 years, studying water quality. Larry lives in North Carolina with his wife, Diane.